The JOURNEY

An Introspective Guide to Your Life and Career Path

Kendall Hunt
publishing company

Patricia Ferguson
Victoria Nanos

Cover photo © Shutterstock, Inc.

Kendall Hunt
publishing company

www.kendallhunt.com
Send all inquiries to:
4050 Westmark Drive
Dubuque, IA 52004-1840

Copyright © 2007, 2009, 2010, 2014, 2016 by Patricia Ferguson and Vicki Nanos

PAK ISBN: 978-1-5249-7512-8
TEXT ALONE ISBN: 978-1-5249-7514-2

Kendall Hunt Publishing Company has the exclusive rights to reproduce this work,
to prepare derivative works from this work, to publicly distribute this work,
to publicly perform this work and to publicly display this work.

All rights reserved. No part of this publication may be reproduced,
stored in a retrieval system, or transmitted, in any form or by any
means, electronic, mechanical, photocopying, recording, or otherwise,
without the prior written permission of the copyright owner.

Printed in the United States of America

contents

Preface v

CHAPTER 1
Introduction 1

Part I: Leaving Home 7

CHAPTER 2
The Search Is On: The Meaning
of Life 9

CHAPTER 3
Climbing the Motivation Pyramid
to Self-Actualization 13

Part II: Trials and Tribulations......19

CHAPTER 4
Who's in Control?......21

CHAPTER 5
Self-Empowerment: Self-Esteem......35

CHAPTER 6
The Emotional You: The Importance of Emotional Intelligence......47
Daniel Goleman, Introduction "Aristotle's Challenge" and Chapter One "What Are Emotions For?"......53

CHAPTER 7
The Social You: Social Intelligence and Diversity......65

Part III: Looking Within......83

CHAPTER 8
Personality Type and You......85
MBTI's Personality Types with Correlating Careers......93
SUIT Yourself: The Secret of Career Satisfaction......97

CHAPTER 9
Connecting the Dots: Interests and Values......103

Part IV: Finding Your Bliss......111

CHAPTER 10
Thinking Clearly: Critical Thinking and Decision Making......113

CHAPTER 11
The Integrated You: Mind, Body, and Spirit......123

CHAPTER 12
The Journey's End......135
Steps to the Hero's Journey Career Exploration Process......138

APPENDIX
Résumé/Cover Letters/Interviewing Process......139

Authors' Biographies......157

preface

The Hero's Journey differs from many life and career purpose books in several fundamental ways. In structuring the book, we have (1) taken a "whole person" view in the design of the content, (2) aligned all the topics with the four elements of the hero's journey, as defined by Joseph Campbell, and (3) included thought-provoking concepts that are in critical thinking.

The "whole person" approach focuses on the internal landscape of the person. It is internally directed and operates on the premise that everything *"out there"* begins with understanding what is going on *"inside."* The whole person view enables you to gain insight into your own nature and to make better choices on "best fit" careers.

The elements of the hero's journey are metaphors for progressive aspects of the developmental states of human growth, motivation, and career decision making. Through the exploration of these elements, you will discover and understand enough about yourself that you will be able to identify your "bliss" and the path you need to follow to obtain it.

We have included chapters on emotional intelligence, social intelligence, diversity, and critical thinking to address the abilities you will need to have when you enter, or re-enter the current job market. We devote an entire chapter on Mind, Body and Spirit with a strong focus on intuition. The twenty-first-century workplace requires more skills than any generation in the past. These skills go well beyond simply having the skills required to perform the duties and functions of a particular job.

The world has become a global village connected by the speed of information processing via the Internet. While our whole person approach involves looking inward, we also need to look out there to be in tune with the interpersonal skills needed to succeed in an increasingly diverse world. We hope that be the end of this book you will discover your bliss and your passion in life.

Patricia Ferguson
Victoria Nanos
April 2016

Additional Notes from the authors:
Interesting movies that correlate with The Hero's Journey: "The Secret" and "What the Bleep Do We Know."

chapter 1

Introduction

> *"You nourish your soul by fulfilling your destiny."*
>
> –Harold Kushner

Image © Krivosheev Vitaly, 2014. Used under license from Shutterstock, Inc.

The famed scholar and mythologist Joseph Campbell (1904–1987) urged us all to "follow our bliss." What does that mean? In its truest form, it means to find your passion and live it. Campbell once said:

If you follow your bliss, you will always have bliss, money or not. If you follow money, you may lose it, and you will have nothing.

Helping you find your passion is one of the main objectives of this book. The capacity for bliss is within each of us. It is buried under layers of self-doubt, peer and family pressure, social demands, and many other deterrents that stop us from finding our bliss. Therefore, it is necessary to peel away those layers and look underneath (or within) to find your passion. Once you have identified your passion, you will devise a plan to integrate that passion into your life to achieve "bliss."

Campbell states one way of finding bliss is to study the "Hero's Journey" or "Hero's Myth." It is a story that is timeless. In going back to stories (myths) thousands of years old, you can see the same pattern, the same story, told repeatedly. From the *Odyssey*, written around 800 B.C., to *Star Wars*, which was written in the late twentieth century, the hero's story stays the same.

The hero's myth generally incorporates following themes:
- The hero leaves home by either choice or force.
- The hero experiences trials and tribulations along the way and learns more about oneself.
- The hero will symbolically experience going down to the underworld (looking within).
- The hero will make a decision to follow a certain path, and in turn, find inner bliss.

FIGURE 1.1: Moses coming down the Mount Sinai

There are many myths and historical stories that could be used to illustrate the hero's myth. Going back 2,500 years, the list is endless: Moses, Buddha, Muhammad, Jesus, David, Mary, Joan of Arc, Krishna, Hercules, Isis, and King Arthur, to name a few.

To further illustrate the hero's myth, take notice of the similarities between these legendary religious figures. After leaving home and experiencing trials and tribulations, they all **looked within** to find out what their destination would be.
- Moses goes up Mount Sinai and returns transformed with the Ten Commandments.

FIGURE 1.2: Muslims awaiting their their turn to pray at the Cave of Hira

FIGURE 1.4: Resurrection of Jesus Christ

FIGURE 1.3: Statue of Buddha under the Bodhi tree

- Muhammad retreats to a mountain cave, known as the cave of Hira, and receives revelations.
- Buddha sits under the Bodhi tree and has an awakening.
- Jesus is crucified and "descends into Hell (Hades) and on the third day" arises and is resurrected.

They all retreated to a place in which they looked inward—a place that led them to their transformation and their bliss.

The Following Synopsis from Homer's *Odyssey* Illustrates the Four Main Themes of the Hero's Myth

LEAVING HOME

Odysseus is forced to leave his home and fight a war in Troy. He spends ten years fighting and defeating the Trojans, and then heads back home to his wife and son in Ithaca. Along the way, Poseidon, the god of the sea, rebukes Odysseus for not acknowledging the help he has received from the gods. Odysseus claims he did everything himself because he is full of vanity, pride, and arrogance. He promises to make it home to Ithaca despite Poseidon's warnings.

TRIALS AND TRIBULATIONS

Odysseus and his men encounter their first crisis when they meet the one-eyed giant. Successfully vanquishing the giant, Odysseus mocks Poseidon again. Later he meets the god of wind who gives Odysseus a sack and tells him not to open it until he and his crew reach Ithaca. However, Odysseus' crew does not heed this warning and they open the sack. As a consequence, they are sent farther from their homeland of Ithaca.

FIGURE 1.5: Odysseus leaves Ithaca

Ultimately, they find themselves on another island where the reigning goddess turns the crew into animals. They stay on that island for five years reduced to pursuing the most basic of human needs: food, drink, and sex.

LOOKING WITHIN

After Odysseus and his crew leave this island, he travels to the underworld to see the blind seer, Teiresias, who tells Odysseus that the way home has been there the whole time; he just needs to see it. Odysseus and his crew face more crises, he loses his entire crew, and ends up on another island with another woman. When he finally realizes that he is a prisoner of his own desires, he makes the decision to return home to Ithaca.

FINDING HIS BLISS

Having made the decision to go home, he builds a ship and designs an escape plan. Odysseus returns home, and the goddess Athena turns him into an old beggar, stripped of all worldly possessions and social status, so he can determine if his wife still wants him after twenty years. He wins back his wife and is transformed into his natural self. He has finally found his bliss.

The Hero's Journey and You

LEAVING HOME

We leave home physically or metaphorically. Whether it is returning to the work force, beginning a new life again after a loss of a partner through divorce or death, transitioning from the military back to civilian life, starting or returning to college, or orienting yourself to gender identification.

TRAILS AND TRIBULATIONS

The expression, "we are our own worst enemy," is the mantra for this section. From our perception of the world through our eyes, we can have an external or internal Locus of Control. Our self-esteem or self-worth, if less than stellar, can be a deterrent for us. How well we control our emotional addictions and our emotional intelligence, can determine our success in our careers and our lives. Our social intelligence and understanding and tolerance of diversity can also determine our success in our careers and our lives.

All of your trails and tribulations are only controlled by one person—you. Other people and certain circumstances may put speed bumps in front of you, but you are the only one who can put up a wall.

LOOKING WITHIN

Fortunately, we will not have to visit the underworld like Odysseus in order to look within and learn about ourselves. For decades, personality and interests' assessments have been used in companies for their employees to understand themselves better or to figure out which employee should be in which job. Career counselors use them to help someone discover their best fit career. Each year dozens of conferences have some sort of break-out session featuring a personality test. Discovering your personality, interests, and values can lead to defining the best fit career or life style for you.

FINDING YOUR BLISS

In addition to looking within, understanding and utilizing critical thinking and decision-making skills can help put together all the information you have gathered. Remember to listen to your intuition to verify or solidify your decision.

Finally, understanding how the mind, body, and spirit are interconnected can help make your transition a smooth one that is full of joy.

"You are never too old to set another goal or to dream a new dream."—C.S. Lewis

FIGURE 1.6

Photo by Scott Kelly.

REFERENCES AND RECOMMENDED READINGS

Campbell, J. (1972). *Myths to Live By*. New York: Bantam Books.
Campbell, J. (1988). *The Power of Myth*. New York: Doubleday.
Leeming, D.A. (1981). *Mythology: The Voyage of the Hero*. New York: Harper Collins.
Osbon, D.K. (1991). *Reflections on the Art of Living: A Joseph Campbell Companion*. New York: Harper Perennial.

Reflective FOCUS

▼ Do you recognize the four themes of the hero's myth in your life?

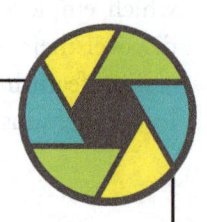

CHAPTER 1: Introduction

PART I

Leaving Home

Odysseus is forced to leave his home and fight a war in Troy. He spends ten years fighting and defeating the Trojans, and then heads back home to his wife and son. Along the way, Poseidon, the god of the sea, rebukes Odysseus for not acknowledging the help he received from the gods. Odysseus claims he did everything himself (he is full of vanity, pride, and arrogance). He says he will make it home to Ithaca despite Poseidon's warnings.

As you metaphorically "leave home," you will continue to search for the meaning of life, look for the motivation needed to obtain bliss and discover your place on Maslow's Hierarchy of Needs and Self-Actualization.

PART I: Leaving Home

chapter 2
The Search Is On

THE MEANING OF LIFE

What brings meaning to your life?

"He who has a why to live can bear with almost any how."

–Nietzsche

The Question Arises as to Which Comes First, the Meaning of Life or the Motivation?

In his book, *Man's Search for Meaning*, Viktor Frankl illustrates how someone who endured the most horrific, brutal, and demoralizing atrocities of a concentration camp found a reason to live, a meaning for his life, and the motivation to go on despite the bleakness of his future.

Frankl shows us that meaning is essential to motivation (in its most basic form, survival). He states that once one finds meaning in life, one becomes stronger spiritually; and once one is stronger spiritually, one is more motivated to survive. Viktor Frankl, one of the most

9

gifted psychiatrists of the twentieth century, reflected on his experiences in a World War II concentration camp, and developed a new thread of psychology called logotherapy. Frankl stated that logotherapy "focuses on the future, that is to say, on the meanings to be fulfilled by the patient in his future."

In the concentration camp, Frankl's motivation to survive was his strong desire to bear witness to the things he had seen, so he could later share those memories with the world. This paragraph from Frankl's book illustrates the connection between spiritual strength and the motivation to survive:

> *Sensitive people who were used to a rich intellectual life may have suffered much pain (they were often of a delicate constitution), but the damage to their inner selves was less. They were able to retreat from the terrible surroundings to a life of inner riches and spiritual freedom. (Frankl, 1959)*

Even simple motivations can be explained in terms of meaning. For example, the decision to mow the lawn or not—if there is no meaning in it for the person doing the mowing, why bother? However, if the person contemplating this job has a strong value of beauty and aesthetics, then the motivation to beautify the yard would have sufficient meaning.

Existential Vacuum

Frankl coined the term "the existential vacuum" to describe the state in which a person finds himself when there is no meaning to his life. It appears as a state of boredom. Sometimes the inability to find real meaning in life is supplanted by the false meaning of **will to power, will to money,** or **will to pleasure.** The will to power, money, and pleasure do not endure as a basis for meaning and motivation in one's life. More often than not, the will to power, money, and pleasure result in feelings of emptiness and frustration.

These substitutes for meaning can never be satisfied and will only result in a desire for more, either with serious, unforgiving consequences like crime, drugs, foreclosures, bankruptcies, prison, and infidelity. Even if these substitutes can be obtained and sustained, still can lead to an unfulfilled, depressing, and lonely life.

For example, a person is given a position of power and, in turn, uses this feeling of power to bring meaning to his or her life. However, once the power is taken away (e.g., the person gets fired or is demoted), the meaning of life also vanishes. The same thing will happen to those who use will to money or will to pleasure to create meaning in life. Once it is taken away, the meaning of life also goes with it.

Frankl believed the existential vacuum was the malady of the twentieth century. He postulated that the root of depression, addiction, and aggression was the existential vacuum.

Fast-forward a few decades to Dale Parnell's *The Neglected Majority*. In his book about community colleges and high school students, Dr. Parnell contends that if students do not have a specific goal in sight, their motivation to complete a degree (or high school diploma) is virtually nonexistent. Of all the students who drop out of high school, 63% are on a general track, with no plans for college or a vocational program; compared to only 6% of those who had plans for college. Therefore: no meaning = no motivation.

Motivation and You

The central theme of this book is finding that goal, that "bliss," and devising a plan to obtain it. Finding the meaning in your life will strengthen your motivation. The chapter on motivation and self-actualization will clarify the development of motivation and its relation to the hero's journey. In the chapter on emotional intelligence, the integral role of emotions on motivation will be explored.

There are multiple factors that impact motivation. You can assimilate the information related to each factor one step at a time. As you master each component, you begin to realize that you have found meaning, value, and emotional commitment, and have established motivation, which will lead you on a smoother road to "bliss."

The true beauty of understanding the elements of motivation is that you will always have control over the ability to motivate yourself. In closing, here is a profound observation by Frankl:

> *We who lived in concentration camps can remember the men who walked through the huts comforting others, giving away their last piece of bread. They may have been few in number, but they offer sufficient proof that everything can be taken from a man but one thing: the last of the human freedoms- to choose one's attitude in any given set of circumstances, to choose one's own way. (Frankl, 1959)*

REFERENCES AND RECOMMENDED READINGS

Frankl, V. (1959). *Man's Search for Meaning*. New York: Simon & Schuster.
Parnell, D. (1993). *The Neglected Majority*. Washington, DC: Community College Press.

Reflective FOCUS

▼ How does "the existential vacuum" hinder us from finding meaning in our lives?

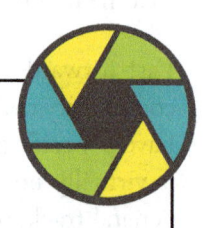

chapter 3
Climbing the Motivation Pyramid to Self-Actualization

"A musician must make music, an artist must paint, a poet must write, if he is to be ultimately at peace with himself. What a man can be, he must be."

–Abraham Maslow

Image © abstrand, 2014. Used under license from Shutterstock, Inc.

In his book *Motivation and Personality*, Abraham Maslow explains his theory of humanistic psychology. He claims that humans strive to reach their highest level of potential, namely self-actualization. This is caused by innate motivation. In order to reach this stage, Maslow says humans need to go through a hierarchy of needs in order to reach self-actualization.

Hierarchy of Needs

The hierarchy begins on the bottom with the most basic human needs, and then progresses to higher level needs. On the first rung are the "having needs" which includes physiological needs—food, water, and shelter—and safety needs—stability, security, and freedom from fear. On the second rung are the "doing needs" which includes sense of belonging and love needs; and self-esteem needs. On the last rung, the top level of the hierarchy is self-actualization—the "being need."

Self-actualization is the final yet ongoing stage. Maslow contended that a person who has self-actualized must follow his or her "calling"—in other words, their bliss.

FIGURE 3.1: Maslow's Hierarchy of Needs

HAVING NEEDS

In the "having needs" our main concern is to take care of our immediate, human needs – the physiological needs – food, water, shelter, clothing and sleep. Things we need in order to live; even a most basic existence. This base of the hierarchy of needs pyramid must be met before we can achieve a higher level of being.

The "safety and security" level is also a having need. Here the main concern is freedom from fear, health, employment to sustain ourselves and our family, and the social ability to live in a society safely.

Once we are comfortable with these two levels, we can focus on the "doing needs" which begin with love and a sense of belonging, and then self-esteem.

However, many people are stuck in the "having needs." This is where addictions begin to occur, especially to food, alcohol, drugs, sex, money, fame, and pride. These addictions hinder people from self-actualization. All individuals partake in "having needs"; but when those needs become their "master," then they will be stuck in that level. This is something akin to Frankl's existential vacuum.

DOING NEEDS

Once individuals master that level and move on to the "doing needs" in the "sense of belonging and love" level, they must shake off any negative feelings they have of themselves and allow others to love them. By allowing others to love them, they embrace and feel a sense of belonging. If they get stuck in this level, they have the propensity to find that sense of belonging in a negative environment, such as gangs or cults. Terrorist organizations target young men (and now women also) who are looking for that sense of belonging. Even though they are doing destructive acts, they feel that they belong to something larger than themselves. If this becomes the case, they cannot begin to obtain self-esteem because the sense of belonging and love is false and negative. The sense of belonging and love must come from a healthy and positive environment. A person can start building self-esteem through obtaining achievements and exhibiting respect for others and self.

Self-esteem is the second level of the "doing needs." Self-esteem can be obtained by gaining mastery in something, by being recognized and respected, or by having confidence and a sense of achievement. This level can usually be mastered several ways; when we start working, join the military, get married, or start taking care of someone, whether it is financially or nurturing or both.

Self-Actualization

Once a person has mastered all the levels, they enter the "being need" and can begin to self-actualize. The following is Maslow's definition of self-actualization:

> *He has within him a pressure toward unity of personality, toward spontaneous expressiveness, toward full individuality and identity, toward seeing the truth rather than being blind, toward being creative, toward being good, and a lot else. That is, the human being is so constructed that he presses toward what most people would call good values, toward serenity, kindness, courage, honesty, love, unselfishness, and goodness. (Maslow, 1968)*

According to Maslow, there are **thirteen attributes for self-actualization**. They are as follows:

1. **Superior perception of reality.** The individual will have an efficient perception of reality, with an exceptional ability to reason.

2. **Increased acceptance of self, of others, and of nature.** The individual will see human nature as it is for self or others.

3. **Increased spontaneity.** The individual will be spontaneous in thoughts and impulses, unhampered by convention. He or she will be motivated by continual growth.

4. **Increase in problem-centering.** Individuals will focus on problems outside of themselves. They will have a mission in life that will be the reason for their existence.

FIGURE 3.2: Self-Actualization

5. **Increased detachment and desire for privacy.** Individuals can be alone, but not lonely. They will be responsible for themselves, and their own behavior.

6. **Increased autonomy and resistance to enculturation.** Individuals are strong within themselves. They are self-contained, and able to withstand peer pressure and obstacles without losing their integrity.

FIGURE 3.3: Greater freshness of appreciation

7. **Greater freshness of appreciation, and richness of emotional reaction.** The individual will have an appreciation for all things and their beauty, and will live in the present moment.

8. **Higher frequency of peak experiences.** Maslow's definition of peak experiences: Feelings of limitless horizons opening up to the vision, the feeling of being simultaneously more powerful and also more helpless than one ever was before, the feeling of ecstasy and wonder and awe, the loss of placement in time and space with, finally, the conviction that something extremely important and valuable has happened, so that the subject was to some extent transformed and strengthened even in his daily life by such experiences. (Maslow, 1968)

9. **Increased identification with the human species.** The individual will have sympathy and affection for mankind and fellowship with all types of people, regardless of gender, race, or social status. Truth will be clearer.

10. **Changed (the clinician would say, improved) interpersonal relations.** The individual will not only have profound, intimate relations with a select few, but will also be capable of greater love.

11. **More democratic character structure.** The individual will be humble, and able to learn from anyone with a strong sense of fairness for all mankind.
12. **Greatly increased creativeness.** Individuals will have an inborn uniqueness that will carry over into everything they do. They will also be more inventive and less inhibited.
13. **Certain changes in the value system.** The individual will be more accepting of a person's nature, of human nature, of social life, and of nature and physical reality. Values will become universal and centered on the good of others, rather than for the good of self.

Motivation — Hierarchy of Needs — Self-Actualization and You

It is the "innate motivation of man" that will lead you to self-actualization in order to reach your highest potential, and live more fully. In living more fully, you not only find your bliss, but also the ability to embrace all parts of yourself, both negative and positive. It is the ultimate feeling of wholeness.

Even though you may feel stuck in one of the "doing" or "having needs," the more you practice (or live) self-actualization, the less pull the "lower level needs" will have on you. In addition, your relationships with family and friends will improve. Your self-esteem will get stronger as your journey to your bliss unfolds.

REFERENCES AND RECOMMENDED READINGS:

Maslow, A. (1970). *Motivation and Personality* (2nd ed.). New York: Harper & Row.
Maslow, A. (1968). *Toward a Psychology of Being*. New York: Van Nostrand Reinhold.

Reflective FOCUS

▼ Where are you on the pyramid; and what do you think you need to do to move up?

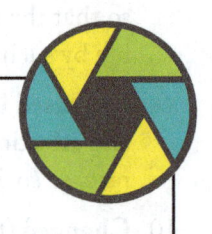

PART I: Leaving Home

PART II
Trials and Tribulations

Odysseus and his men encounter their first crisis when they meet the one-eyed giant. Successfully vanquishing the giant, Odysseus mocks Poseidon again. Later he meets the god of wind, and the god gives Odysseus a sack and tells him not to open it until they reach Ithaca. However, Odysseus' crew does not heed this warning and they open the sack. As a consequence, they are sent farther from their homeland of Ithaca.

During Part II "trials and tribulations," you will discover the limitations of having an external locus of control, and the benefits of having an internal locus of control. You will also look at your self-esteem, discovering how it has negatively or positively impacted your life and choices. Throughout this process of introspection, you will create ways to develop a stronger sense of self and a feeling of empowerment.

As you become aware of your emotional intelligence quotient (EQ) and the challenges associated with a low EQ, you will begin to understand how handling emotions inappropriately can hinder the attainment of your bliss. Social intelligence and diversity are introduced and examined, highlighting the ways you can enhance your ability to interact with others.

Image © Angela Waye, 2014. Used under license from Shutterstock, Inc.

PART II: Trials and Tribulations

chapter 4
Who's in Control?

"People's misfortunes result from mistakes they make."

"Many of the unhappy things in people's lives are partly due to bad luck."

–Julian Rotter

Image © scyther5, 2014. Used under license from Shutterstock, Inc.

In this section, two psychological theories will be discussed. Locus of control (LOC) theory, and William Glasser's choice theory. Both are cognitive theories that address the issues of external locus of control, choices, rational thought processes, and the impact they have on individuals.

Locus of Control

The first theory we explore is locus of control. The two statements under the title of this section represent the two polarities of the locus of control theory. Locus of control is a social learning theory first hypothesized by psychologist Julian Rotter. The term refers to a person's perception that he or she is in control of life's events.

Rotter determined that people display either external locus of control (ELOC) or internal locus of control (ILOC). The first statement above reflects an ILOC. ILOC people believe that events are controlled by internal factors, and that they have the ability to control and bring about change in their behaviors and life's events.

The second statement is one that a person with ELOC would make. ELOC people believe that behavior and events in life are influenced by outside events beyond their control. They take the position that events happen as a result of other people. For example, the person who states: "It's not my fault that I couldn't pay my electric bill on time. I had to help my boyfriend move," has an ELOC orientation.

Another theorist, Hanna Levenson, expanded LOC theory to include three distinct categories: internal locus of control, powerful others, and chance control. According to Levenson, individuals can display one of the categories to a great degree, or a combination of all three. Powerful others is equated with ELOC, and the idea that other people have more influence on a person's behaviors and decisions than the person themselves. Chance control would include the impact of acts of nature (tornadoes, hurricanes, and earthquakes), fate, destiny, and belief in a God that takes away free will.

FIGURE 4.1: Chance Control

People with ILOC are thought to fare better in life. Having an ILOC creates a positive impact on physical and mental health. Persons with ILOC persist longer to complete tasks, and are more likely to benefit from extensive instructions to finish a task.

Internal locus of control matches up with Maslow's fifth attribute of self-actualization: *"Increased detachment and need for privacy. Individuals can be alone, but not lonely. They will be responsible for themselves and their own behavior."* People with an internal locus of control do not need others around to make them feel good. They are comfortable being alone. That is not to say that they do not desire the company of others, only that they are more discriminating in their choice. Instead of spending time with fair-weather friends, they desire and choose privacy. Along with increased detachment from others, comes responsibility for one's own behavior and the decision not to be a "pawn" for others. They have distaste for hypocritical and phony people and opt not to associate with them.

Those with an ELOC tend to procrastinate, and finish tasks late. They are easily frustrated and discouraged by detailed instructions.

Though Rotter believed individuals have a genetic predisposition for a particular locus of control, it is thought that a person's societal interactions can change their locus of control orientation. After all, if LOC is based on an individual's perception of control, then clearly they can alter their perceptions at any stage of life.

Choice Theory

William Glasser developed choice theory as a way to understand and assist individuals who were experiencing difficulties in their lives. Glasser contended that for all practical purposes, people choose everything they do, even the unhappiness they feel, and that no other person can make them happy or miserable. All that anyone can get from another person is information, and that is all that can be given.

The choices that individuals make and the subsequent actions that a person may take as a result of those choices yield a particular experience; therefore, if individuals do not like the outcome of a specific choice, they have only themselves to blame. Glasser argued that most people do not own up to the responsibility for their choices, but point to external factors (I was late for work because some cop pulled me over for speeding) as the cause of their misery. External factors equal external locus of control as described in the earlier segment of this section.

FIGURE 4.2: Choice Theory

Glasser hypothesized that the choices a person makes are generated from a place of basic needs and feelings. He cited that individuals have basic needs for the following: (1) survival; (2) love, loving sex, and belonging (human beings want to be in relationships with others); (3) power (human beings want to have influence over others); (4) freedom (the paradox that while human beings want to be in relationships with others, they also want private space to be who they are); and (5) fun (human beings like to play). Glasser's basic needs and feelings line up very nicely with several of Maslow's Hierarchy of Needs: the physiological needs, love and belonging, and self-esteem.

In terms of these basic needs, all people have greater or lesser needs in each area. Therefore, the choices a person makes are directly linked to how important a particular need is to that individual. According to Glasser, the overall desire of most people is to be happy, and to be in relationships with others. Choice theory can become a tightrope walk. How do you make choices that honor your own needs, and yet not alienate you from others or your own happiness?

Glasser's advice is to first accept that you cannot control anyone else's behavior but your own. Choice theory states that if a person can make one choice, then he or she can make an alternate choice. For example, a person maybe feeling unhappy and choose to wallow in misery (which is a passive acceptance of unhappiness), or the person can choose to think about misery in a different way ("my unhappiness is telling me something important") and choose an action that will move him or her through the feeling ("I will talk to my best friend" or "I will go work out in the gym").

Choice theory dictates that individuals should ask themselves the following questions: "How will the choice I make in this moment bring me closer to others?" "How does this choice meet my basic needs?" "What do I need to do to ensure I move toward happiness?"

LOC and You

In identifying your locus of control, and coupling the information with Glasser's choice theory, you have a powerful tool at your disposal. The proper application of this tool can empower you to realize that you, not others, have the power to choose your direction in life. The choices won't always be easy, but the process of choosing will become empowering.

We will close out this chapter with a poem written by the nineteenth-century poet, William Ernest Henley, titled "Invictus." Mr. Henley wrote the poem about the challenge he faced when he contracted a form of polio as a young boy that required him to have his leg amputated. This poem illustrates the choice that is before all of us, each and every time we are faced with a trying situation or obstacle: the choice to be controlled by the challenge presented to us OR to take our fate in our own hands, learn from our trials and tribulations, and continue on our journey toward bliss.

Levenson's Locus-of-Control Assessment

Instructions

Use the following scale; indicate your level of agreement or disagreement with each of the statements listed below:

4 = Strongly Agree
3 = Agree
2 = Disagree
1 = Strongly Disagree

1. Whether or not I get to be a leader depends on my ability.
   - ○ Strongly Agree (4)
   - ○ Agree (3)
   - ○ Disagree (2)
   - ○ Strongly Disagree (1)

2. To a great extent, my life is controlled by accidental happenings.
   - ○ Strongly Agree (4)
   - ○ Agree (3)
   - ○ Disagree (2)
   - ○ Strongly Disagree (1)

3. I feel what happens in my life is mostly determined by powerful people.
   - ○ Strongly Agree (4)
   - ○ Agree (3)
   - ○ Disagree (2)
   - ○ Strongly Disagree (1)

4. Whether or not I get into a car accident depends mainly on how good a driver I am.
   - Strongly Agree (4)
   - Agree (3)
   - Disagree (2)
   - Strongly Disagree (1)

5. When I make plans, I am almost certain to make them work.
   - Strongly Agree (4)
   - Agree (3)
   - Disagree (2)
   - Strongly Disagree (1)

6. Often there is no chance of protecting my personal interest from bad luck happening.
   - Strongly Agree (4)
   - Agree (3)
   - Disagree (2)
   - Strongly Disagree (1)

7. When I get what I want, it's usually because I am lucky.
   - Strongly Agree (4)
   - Agree (3)
   - Disagree (2)
   - Strongly Disagree (1)

8. Although I might have good ability, I will not be given leadership responsibility without appealing to those in positions of power.
   - Strongly Agree (4)
   - Agree (3)
   - Disagree (2)
   - Strongly Disagree (1)

9. How many friends I have depends on how nice a person I am.
   - ○ Strongly Agree (4)
   - ○ Agree (3)
   - ○ Disagree (2)
   - ○ Strongly Disagree (1)

10. I have often found that what is going to happen will happen.
    - ○ Strongly Agree (4)
    - ○ Agree (3)
    - ○ Disagree (2)
    - ○ Strongly Disagree (1)

11. My life is chiefly controlled by powerful others.
    - ○ Strongly Agree (4)
    - ○ Agree (3)
    - ○ Disagree (2)
    - ○ Strongly Disagree (1)

12. Whether I get in to a car accident is mostly a matter of luck.
    - ○ Strongly Agree (4)
    - ○ Agree (3)
    - ○ Disagree (2)
    - ○ Strongly Disagree (1)

13. People like me have very little chance of protecting our personal interests when they conflict with those of strong pressure groups.
    - ○ Strongly Agree (4)
    - ○ Agree (3)
    - ○ Disagree (2)
    - ○ Strongly Disagree (1)

14. It's not always wise for me to plan too far ahead because many things turn out to be a matter of good or bad fortune.
    - Strongly Agree (4)
    - Agree (3)
    - Disagree (2)
    - Strongly Disagree (1)

15. Getting what I want requires pleasing people above me.
    - Strongly Agree (4)
    - Agree (3)
    - Disagree (2)
    - Strongly Disagree (1)

16. Whether or not I get to be a leader depends on whether I am lucky enough to be in the right place at the right time.
    - Strongly Agree (4)
    - Agree (3)
    - Disagree (2)
    - Strongly Disagree (1)

17. If important people were to decide they didn't like me, I probably wouldn't make many friends.
    - Strongly Agree (4)
    - Agree (3)
    - Disagree (2)
    - Strongly Disagree (1)

18. I can pretty much determine what will happen in my life.
    - ○ Strongly Agree (4)
    - ○ Agree (3)
    - ○ Disagree (2)
    - ○ Strongly Disagree (1)

19. I am usually able to protect my personal interests.
    - ○ Strongly Agree (4)
    - ○ Agree (3)
    - ○ Disagree (2)
    - ○ Strongly Disagree (1)

20. Whether or not I get into a car accident depends mainly on the other driver.
    - ○ Strongly Agree (4)
    - ○ Agree (3)
    - ○ Disagree (2)
    - ○ Strongly Disagree (1)

21. When I get what I want, it's usually because I worked for it.
    - ○ Strongly Agree (4)
    - ○ Agree (3)
    - ○ Disagree (2)
    - ○ Strongly Disagree (1)

22. In order to have my plans work, I make sure that they fit in with the desires of people who have power over me.
    - ○ Strongly Agree (4)
    - ○ Agree (3)
    - ○ Disagree (2)
    - ○ Strongly Disagree (1)

23. My life is determined by my own actions.
    - ○ Strongly Agree (4)
    - ○ Agree (3)
    - ○ Disagree (2)
    - ○ Strongly Disagree (1)

24. It's chiefly a matter of fate whether or not I have a few or many friends.
    - ○ Strongly Agree (4)
    - ○ Agree (3)
    - ○ Disagree (2)
    - ○ Strongly Disagree (1)

SCORING: Add up your score for the following groups of questions.
Internal Control: Questions 1, 4, 5, 9, 18, 19, 21, 23
Chance Control: Questions 2, 6, 7, 10, 12, 14, 16, 24
Powerful Others: 3, 8, 11, 13, 15, 17, 20, 22

Question 1	☐	Question 2	☐	Question 3	☐
Question 4	☐	Question 6	☐	Question 8	☐
Question 5	☐	Question 7	☐	Question 11	☐
Question 9	☐	Question 10	☐	Question 13	☐
Question 18	☐	Question 12	☐	Question 15	☐
Question 19	☐	Question 14	☐	Question 17	☐
Question 21	☐	Question 16	☐	Question 20	☐
Question 23	☐	Question 24	☐	Question 22	☐
Total ILOC	☐	Total CC	☐	Total PO	☐
		Total ELOC (Total CC + Total PO)	☐		

Important: for ELOC score you must add scores from CC (Chance Control) and PO (Powerful Others) together.

Internal Control		Chance Control		Powerful Others	

For the Levenson Locus-of-Control Assessment, your three scores will fall between eight (8) and thirty-two (32). You need to look at your scores on all three scales in relation to one another to determine how you feel about control in your life.

Source: "Activism and Powerful Others: Distinctions within the Concept of Internal-External Control" by H. Levenson from Journal of Personality Assessment 38: 377–383. Copyright © 1974 Routledge. Reprinted by permission of the publisher (Taylor & Francis Ltd, http://www.tandf.co.uk/journals).

Invictus

Out of the night that covers me
Black as the pit from pole to pole.
I thank whatever gods may be
For my unconquerable soul.

In the fell clutch of circumstance
I have not winced nor cried aloud.
Under the bludgeoning of chance
My head is bloody, but unbowed.

Beyond this place of wrath and tears
Looms but the Horror of the shade.
And yet the menace of the years
Finds, and shall find me, unafraid.

> It matters not how strait the gate,
> How charged with punishments the scroll.
> I am master of my fate:
> I am captain of my soul.
>
> —William Ernest Henley

REFERENCES AND RECOMMENDED READINGS:

Glasser, W. (1998). *Choice Theory: A New Psychology of Personal Freedom*. New York: Harper Perennial.

Henley, William Ernest (1888). *A Book of Verses* (3rd ed.). New York: Scribner and Welford.

Lau, R.R. (1982). Origins of health locus of control beliefs. *Journal of Personality and Social Psychology* 42(2): 322–234.

Rotter, J.B. (1971). Internal/external locus of control. *Psychology Today* V(1).

Wallston, K.A., Wallston, B.S., & DeVellis, R. (1978). Development of multidimensional locus of control. *Health Education Monographs*, 160–170.

Reflective FOCUS

▼ What trials and tribulations have you experienced in your life that have influenced the development of your locus of control?

▼ If you allowed circumstances or other people to influence your choices, what could you have done differently to be in control of your life?

chapter 5
Self-Empowerment

SELF-ESTEEM

Image © Jan Felker, 2014. Used under license from Shutterstock, Inc.

"No one can make you feel inferior without your consent."
—Eleanor Roosevelt

"The greatest evil that can befall man is that he should think ill of himself."
—Goethe

Self-empowerment is about your owning your power and taking control of your life. There are several components to empowerment: decision-making power, assertiveness, the ability to express anger appropriately, the ability to gather and process information, the capacity to think clearly and critically, and self-esteem, to name a few. In this chapter we will focus on the self-esteem aspect of empowerment because we believe self-esteem is the foundation for developing self-empowerment.

The subject of self-esteem has been a staple of magazines, books, and TV talk shows in America. In their combined twenty-five-plus years of doing therapy with individuals, the authors of this book have found that the core issue for 90% of the people they counsel is low self-esteem or the feeling of "not being worthy."

Low self-esteem or the feeling of "not being worthy" can interfere with your attempts to reach your goals. For example, the lack of motivation, persistence, or a lack of willingness to take risks that will yield rewards often impede goal attainment. Because of this phenomenon, the authors felt it was critical to include a section on self-esteem in *The Hero's Journey*. Research indicates that there is a strong correlation between high self-esteem and finding one's bliss.

You can be well educated, successful in your career and your relationships, and yet the feeling of not being worthy could still persist. It is no wonder that people spend so much time and money trying to root out the causes of low self-esteem. The need to feel worthy and to be accepted is at the center of being human.

High Self-Esteem

Individuals with high self-esteem tend to be more tolerant and respectful of others, accept responsibility for their actions, and have integrity. They are willing to take risks, can handle criticism, are loving and loveable, and take pride in their successes. As a society, we need and want to develop individuals with healthy levels of self-esteem.

Low Self-Esteem

People with low self-esteem tend to focus on trying to prove themselves or impress others. They generally lack self-confidence, and have doubts about their worth and acceptability. As a result, they are sometimes reluctant to take risks or expose themselves to failure. Individuals with low self-esteem can display a range of behaviors, from being arrogant, to being apologetic and self-effacing. From the authors' experiences, there is a relationship between low self-esteem and problems such as violence, drug abuse, alcoholism, eating disorders, school dropouts, teenage pregnancy, suicide, and low academic achievement. Low self-esteem may not be a **primary cause** of these problems, but it could be a **contributing factor**.

Definition of Self-Esteem

Nathaniel Branden, a well-known author and psychotherapist, defines self-esteem as "the disposition to experience oneself as being competent to cope with the basic challenges of life and being worthy of happiness."

The National Association of Self-Esteem defines self-esteem as "the experience of being capable of meeting life's challenges and of being worthy of happiness." In both definitions, one can see the **dual components of competence and worthiness** as being essential to self-esteem.

Competence and Worthiness

Competence is the sense of having the belief that you are generally capable of producing desired results, having the confidence in your intelligence and ability to think, and to make the right choices and decisions. A simple example would be as follows: Janey buys a cake mix, and believes that she has the ability to read the directions and bake a cake. Another example: John, a recently retired lieutenant in the army is applying for a position at a company. He is confident that he is qualified for the position and that he will do well on the interview because of his experiences in the military and his personal characteristics.

Competence is developed through realistic and accurate self-assessment, meaningful accomplishments, overcoming adversities, recovering from failures, becoming responsible for oneself, and maintaining integrity.

Worthiness might be considered the psychological component of self-esteem. Self-worth is the unconditional value you place on yourself. It is an overall measure of how much you value yourself and give priority to your own needs and happiness. With high self-worth, you love yourself unconditionally in all situations and in all areas of your life. You love yourself even when you make mistakes or do dumb things. You love yourself no matter how bad you think you were, and can allow good things to happen to you without feeling guilty. Here is a story to illustrate this: a well-known actor recounts the time he took a date to see a 3D James Bond movie. He and his date sit down in the darkened theatre and put on their 3D glasses. The actor notices the young women sitting next to him kept looking at him and he thinks it is because they recognize him. So he doesn't make much of it. Then the movie begins and he realizes he is in the wrong theatre. The movie that is showing is "Nanny McPhee." He was too embarrassed to get up and leave the theatre so he and his date sat through the entire movie. The actor is able to tell the story of his mistake with humor and charm that doesn't detract from his sense of self worth.

Healthy self-esteem is a result of the marriage between competence and worthiness—they balance each other. Worthiness prevents competence from turning into arrogance, and competence prevents worthiness from turning into narcissism by requiring that good feelings be earned, not given.

How Does Self-Esteem Develop?

No one is born with high self-esteem. It is **learned behavior** that is the result of a number of influences: family, peers, and society. The family is probably the core source of our feeling of being loved unconditionally or conditionally. In speaking with clients in therapy, it is clear to the authors that in many cases, it is the parents who set the stage for their children's feelings of "not being good enough" by making comparisons between their children and outside others. When parents make statements like "Joanie is the pretty one, and Samantha is the smart one." Or "Why can't you be more like your cousin John? He is so successful." Children tend to internalize comparisons, and as a result they compare themselves to others, and if they have low self-esteem, could find themselves lacking. This alienated feeling usually carries on well beyond childhood.

In addition to the family influence, the plethora of messages the media/society sends to the public about what is acceptable can impact on the development of a positive self-image. Fashion magazines tell women that they should look like the fashion models—tall, thin, and well endowed, and men's magazines tout the well-developed six-pack stomach as the ideal for men. Individuals are bombarded with conflicting messages from a variety of sources. If you have high self-esteem, you are able to withstand the onslaught of those influences because your center of self-worth comes from within.

The good news is that because self-esteem is learned behavior, you can change and develop a better sense of self.

Ways to Improve Self-Esteem

To begin improving self-esteem, you need to accept one basic premise: You are the *only* source of your self-esteem; therefore, you are the *only* one who has the power to make yourself feel good about yourself. No other person can love you enough or compliment you enough to raise your self-esteem. Improving your self-esteem is an internal process.

Most of us have spent a lifetime creating our self-image; so raising our self-esteem will not happen overnight. The process begins by having compassion for ourselves. Compassion for self is at the core of self-esteem. Matthew McKay and Patrick Fanning in their book *Self-Esteem* state:

> *When you have compassion for yourself, you understand and accept yourself. If you make a mistake, you forgive yourself. You have reasonable expectations of yourself. You set attainable goals. You tend to see yourself as basically good.*
>
> *When you learn to feel compassion for yourself, you begin exposing your sense of self-worth . . . Compassionate self-talk can wash away the sediment of hurt and rejection that may have covered your innate self-acceptance for years.*

We often find that the self-talk of people with low self-esteem is very critical and negative. They look in the mirror and say to their own image, "You are ugly"…."Your nose is too big"…"Your eyes are too far apart"…."No one will love you."

Self-esteem is an attitude of compassion, acceptance, and nonjudgment toward self and others.

Words Have Power

Words have the power on a grand scale to change the course of history, to inspire people to believe in something greater than themselves, to right the wrongs of society, and on a smaller scale to raise someone up or crush someone to the ground. To show the power of words, the late Japanese scientist Masaru Emoto, author of The Hidden Messages in Water, conducted an interesting study using water.

FIGURE 5.1

He began his experiments by filling petri dishes with different kinds of water—distilled, spring, river, freshwater lake—and then putting them in a chilling environment to freeze the water. Dr. Emoto would then use a high-powered microscope/camera to photograph the frozen water. The resulting photos showed the different crystal patterns the water from each source formed. The water from a river had a different crystal pattern from the distilled water, which had a different pattern from the freshwater lake, etc.

Dr. Emoto added another element to his experiments by playing different forms of music while he photographed the water samples. To his surprise, the crystal patterns that formed for each water sample varied depending on the type of music that was played.

Dr. Emoto then wondered what would happen if he affixed a word like *love* or *hate* to his water samples and then photograph them. Amazingly, the crystal patterns that developed were vastly different, depending on the word written on the label. The water samples labeled *love* formed large, beautiful, and harmonious crystal patterns. Those labeled with the word *hate* had poorly formed crystal patterns that weren't as appealing as the "love" crystals.

Love and Gratitude

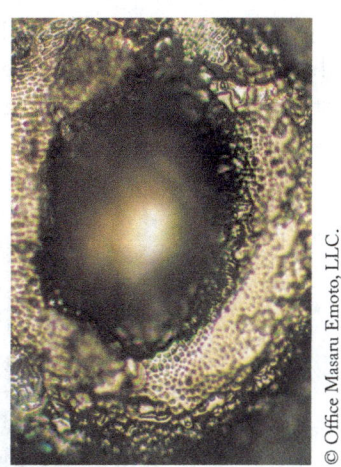

Evil

You disgust me

Thank you

Dr. Emoto also conducted an experiment using three bowls of the same type of rice. On the first bowl, he wrote the word "thank you." On the second bowl, he wrote the word "you're an idiot." The third bowl had no words affixed to it. He left the bowl on a shelf and each day he would say "thank you" to the bowl labeled with those words and he would yell "you're an idiot" to bowl with that label. The third bowl he completely ignored. Dr. Emoto alleged that after a period of time the "you're an idiot" bowl and the ignored bowl started to turn colors. He stated that the "thank you" bowl remained unchanged. At the end of the experiment, Dr. Emoto noted that the ignored bowl turned black with mold the fastest,

CHAPTER 5: SELF-EMPOWERMENT: Self-Esteem

followed by the "you're an idiot" bowl. The "thank you" bowl, according to Emoto remained unchanged. Dr. Emoto concluded from this experiment that though negative words have a deleterious effect on a person/thing, ignoring a person/thing is far worse.

FIGURE 5.2: Emoto – three bowls of rice

The average human body is 70% water. Knowing this fact, Dr. Emoto hypothesized that words, both positive and negative, just as the water crystals dishes showed, can have tremendous power to impact human beings, not only psychologically but physically as well.

If you accept and believe the results of Dr. Emoto's experiments, you have to say to yourself, "If words written on a petri dish filled with water can have an impact on the crystal patterns of water, then imagine what words can do to me and others!"

We have already discussed the power of words earlier in this chapter in terms of the effect our negative self-talk has on our sense of self and the impact the critical words of our loved ones can have on us. And every day, in the media we see the results of bullying whether it is in person or via social media. Some young people doing harm to themselves because of the barrage of words directed at them by others.

So the next time you are tempted to use self-critical words or words to criticize yourself or others, think about Emoto's study and retrain yourself to speak positive and uplifting words.

Go to www.masaru-emoto.net to view the photos: Love and Gratitude, You Make Me Sick, Angel, and Satan.

Specific Ways to Develop Self-Esteem:

1. Don't indulge in self-criticism. Try to stifle the inner voice that judges.
2. Choose to feel good. When needing a boost in confidence try recalling three memories of good times, music, and people's faces that you love.
3. Don't always try to please others. It is good to be considerate of others, but not to the extent of neglecting yourself.
4. Practice acceptance. Acceptance means acknowledging the facts, while suspending judgment.
5. Don't try to be like someone else. Remember the words of the German writer, Goethe: "If God wanted me Otherwise, He would have made me Otherwise." Each person is unique and cannot be someone else.
6. Don't take life, or self, so seriously. Failure is not the end of the world. Becoming a problem-solver can make you stronger.
7. Learn to focus on your own desires and needs. You deserve to live the life you want.
8. Focus on successes. Learn from failures; however leave them in the past.
9. Practice forgiving. Forgiving means letting go of a past incident without dwelling on it or becoming miserable about it all over again. Forgiving does not mean you approve; it merely means the case is closed.
10. Focus on strengths and use them.

To Love oneself is the beginning of a lifelong romance.

—Oscar Wilde

Self-Esteem and You

Maslow's sixth attribute of self-actualization is *"increased autonomy and resistance to enculturation."* In developing this attribute, you have a strong sense of self and can establish definite boundaries (you will know where you end and others begin). You are able to withstand peer pressure and overcome obstacles without losing your integrity. You are self-contained.

Sometimes when people develop this attribute, others often accused them of being aloof and/or detached. This is because such individuals are not swayed by peer pressure and other external influences. They do not need approval from others in terms of the clothes they wear, the career path they follow, or the friends and intimate partners they choose. They are self-contained and therefore autonomous.

FIGURE 5.3

High self-esteem also affects one's resistance to enculturation. Enculturation is defined as a person's inability to maintain his or her own identity in the midst of a dominant culture. Maslow's theory of resistance to enculturation (part of the sixth attribute) describes individuals who keep their identity while surrounded by a dominant culture. They don't play "follow the leader" unless the leader makes sense. They will only protest or fight for something that they know will not be in vain. They choose their battles wisely. This is true empowerment.

The investment you make in developing self-empowerment and raising your self-esteem will return to you a hundredfold. Being empowered and having high self-esteem will not guarantee a perfect, problem-free life, but it will assist you in handling the challenges that life will bring you so that you can be a happier, healthier person, with a positive attitude toward life. By raising your self-esteem, your motivation to persist in achieving your goals becomes stronger and, in turn, supports you in achieving your "bliss."

REFERENCES AND RECOMMENDED READINGS:

Branden, N. (2001). *The Psychology of Self-Esteem.* New York: Jossey-Bass.
Branden, N. (1995). *Six Pillars of Self-Esteem.* New York: Bantam Books.
Branden, N. (1987). *How to Raise Your Self-Esteem.* New York: Bantam Books.
Emoto, M. (2001). *The Hidden Messages in Water.* Oregon: Beyond Words Publishing.
McKay, M., & Fanning, P. (1988). *Self-Esteem: A Proven Program of Cognitive Techniques for Assessing, Improving, and Maintaining Self-Esteem.* New York: St. Martin's Press.

Reflective FOCUS

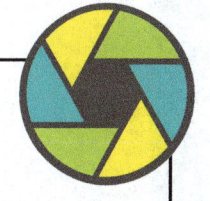

▼ What is the difference between having high self-esteem and being perceived as arrogant?

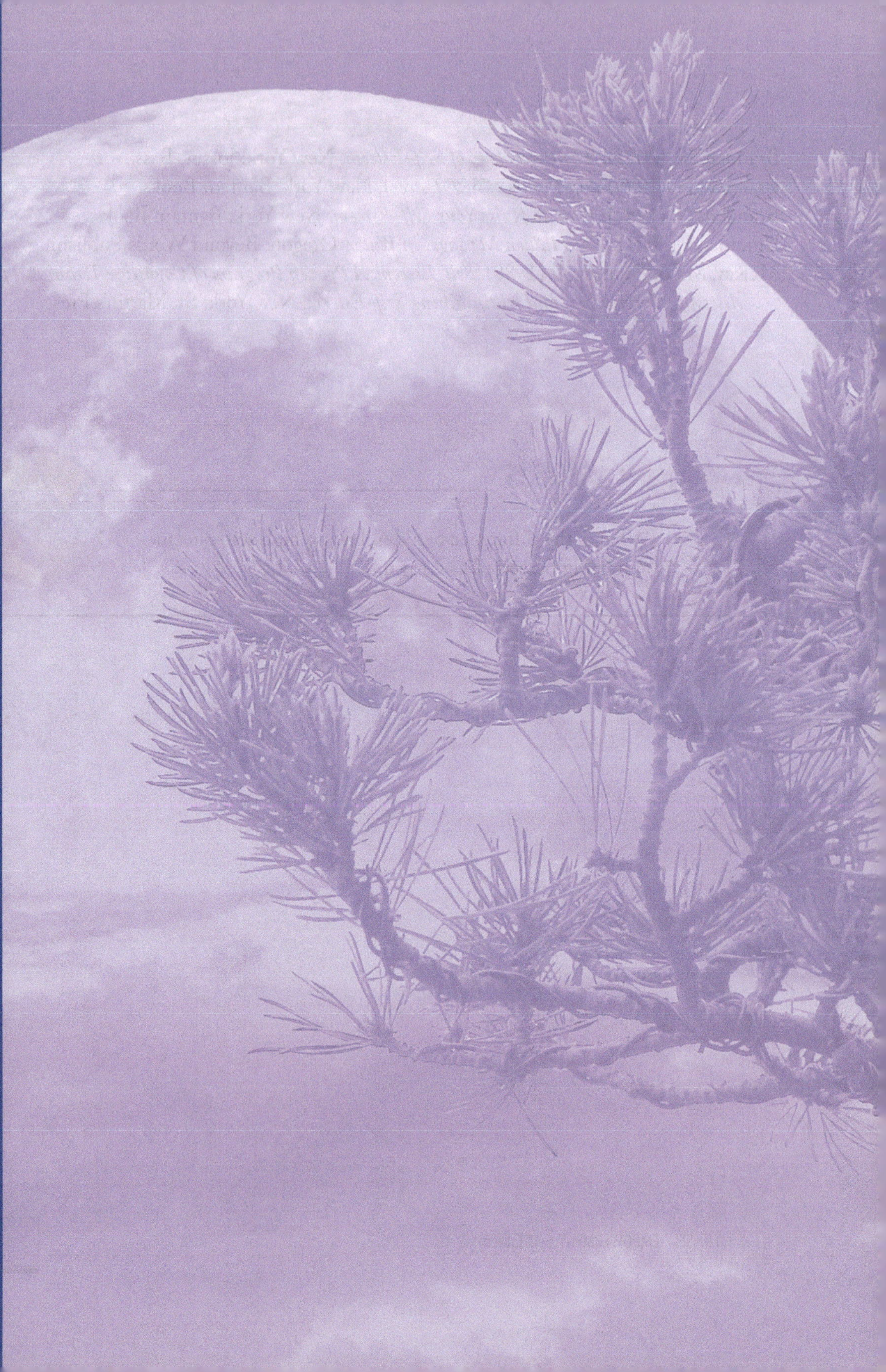

chapter 6
The Emotional You

THE IMPORTANCE OF EMOTIONAL INTELLIGENCE

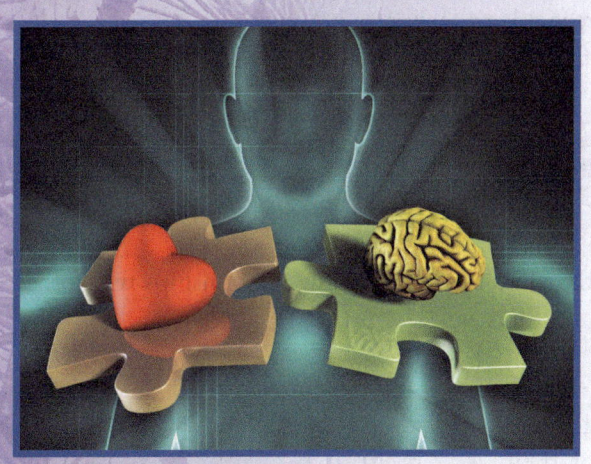

Image © Andrea Danti, 2014. Used under license from Shutterstock, Inc.

"Our greatest weakness lies in giving up. The most certain way to succeed is always to try just one more time."

–Thomas Edison

The name Albert Einstein and genius IQ (intelligence quotient) are synonymous in most people's minds. Today there is a new intelligence measure that rivals IQ; it is called EQ, or emotional intelligence quotient.

Although the term "emotional intelligence (EQ)" was first coined in the 1990s by Peter Salovey and John Mayer, EQ came to the public's attention with the publication of the book *Emotional Intelligence* by Daniel Goleman. Salovey and Mayer (1975) define emotional intelligence as "the ability to express emotion accurately; the ability to understand emotion and emotional knowledge; the ability to access and to generate feelings when they facilitate thought; and the ability to regulate emotions in ways that assist thought."

Through clinical studies, Daniel Goleman has found that EQ is more important than IQ in predicting emotional/physical health, success in relationships, and job performance. In layman's terms, being a genius is not the best predictor of success. However, being emotionally smart gives you a better chance of being successful and happy.

Characteristics of Emotional Intelligence (EQ)

Why is this the case? It appears that emotionally intelligent people, whose IQ can vary from average to genius, share certain characteristics that enhance their ability to live successfully. Emotionally intelligent people tend to:

1. know their feelings and are able to recognize a feeling as it occurs;
2. manage their emotions and handle their feelings in appropriate ways;
3. be able to motivate themselves;
4. persist in the face of frustration;
5. control their impulses and delay gratification;
6. be able to empathize with others;
7. have the capacity to hope; and
8. have social competencies—that is, they know how to handle relationships with other people.

Individuals with EQ also display a "self-aware" style in dealing with their feelings. Self-aware people tend to be autonomous, sure of their boundaries, positive in their outlook on life, and able to get in, or out of, a mood quickly.

Individuals who do not possess EQ, more often than not, let their emotions and moods control them. They become engulfed by their feelings and believe they are helpless to escape them. Relationships with others tend to be tumultuous, because those who lack EQ are unable to accurately read other people's feeling states. They get lost in the swamp of their own emotions and lose their ability to perceive objectively.

FIGURE 6.1: The many faces of emotion

Mind, Body, and Emotions

Through studies, it has been confirmed that mind, body, and emotion form a linked system. Emotions are enmeshed in the neural network of reason (the neocortex section of the human brain). Learning and meaning are driven by feelings. The brain is, in some respects, a box filled with emotions, and it is now known that emotions are the key to motivation.

Emotional Addictions

Scientists who study the biochemistry of emotions have discovered that each emotion has a distinct chemical makeup, and when an emotion is expressed, a receptor site is created on a cell for that emotion. The more often a person expresses that particular emotion (e.g., anger), a corresponding increase in the number of receptor sites and cells occur. A habitual pattern of emotional response (i.e., you always respond in anger when driving your car on a highway) can create an addiction to that emotion, in the same way that a person develops an addiction to nicotine or alcohol. As in the use of nicotine, where the more you smoke, the more you need to smoke, the more you respond to situations/people/events with a particular emotion, the more you wire yourself to that emotion at a biochemical level.

Emotional Intelligence and You

When you create habitual patterns of emotional responses, the following things result: (1) you establish an addiction to particular emotional states; (2) you limit your range of emotional expression; and (3) you react without thinking, and often respond inappropriately to certain situations. The good news is that you can alter your emotional addictions.

Scientists have found that if people interrupt their typical pattern of emotional response, they can shut off a receptor for that emotion. Every time you react differently from your habitual emotional pattern, you inactivate more receptors on more cells until you no longer have an addiction to that particular emotion. Let's go back to the example of driving a car and experiencing road rage when someone cuts in front of you on the highway. The next time a car cuts in front of you, instead of yelling obscenities and raising your fist at the other driver, keep your hands on the wheel and your mouth closed. **You have now taken the first step in interrupting your habitual response.** You may still feel anger, but you have de-escalated its intensity. If you continue to react differently, you will eventually extinguish your trigger to become angry in this situation.

It stands to reason that the more skilled you become at managing your emotions and learning to use them as allies of reason and logic, the more you will be able to live a successful life. This is where emotional intelligence can help you.

In the chapter of Self-actualization we talked about Maslow's tenth attribute for self-actualization: "*Improved interpersonal relationships. You will have profound, intimate relations with a select few. You will be capable of greater love.*" Having emotional intelligence is a precursor for having healthy relationships with others. You can have a few close relationships instead of many superficial ones. When we have EQ, we combine reason, compassion, and logic with our emotions and, in turn, can have healthy relationships and assists us on our journey to self-actualization.

One of the positive aspects of emotional intelligence is that you are not fated by genetic predisposition to have high or low EQ levels. EQ skills can be learned. The key in learning to manage emotions is balance—that is, keeping those distressing emotions in check. Identifying ways to soothe yourself in the face of upsets, frustrations, and stress is a fundamental life skill that will enhance EQ.

The goal of EQ is not focused on suppressing emotions; you need to embrace your feelings. EQ emphasizes the recognition of your emotional state and working with it, while not allowing feelings to overwhelm you. *In the final analysis, it comes down to owning your emotions, and not letting your emotions own you!*

REFERENCES AND RECOMMENDED READINGS:

Bennett-Goleman, T. (2001). *Emotional Alchemy*. New York: Harmony Books.
Goleman, D. (1975). *Emotional Intelligence*. New York: Bantam Books. See excepts below.
Goleman, D. (2013). *Focus: The Hidden Driver of Excellence*. New York: Harper
Salovey, P., & Mayer, J.D. (1990). *Emotional Intelligence: Imagination, Cognition, and Personality*. New York: New York Press.
Simmons, S., & Simmons, J.C. (1997). *Measuring Emotional Intelligence*. Arlington, TX: Summit Publishing Group.

Emotional Intelligence Assessment

Find out how you rate on this Emotional Intelligence Assessment

Rate yourself on a scale from 1–9 on the following statements. 1–3 = not like me; 4–6 = somewhat like me; 7–9 = most like me

* I don't give up easily even when faced with many obstacles. **(persistence)**
○ 1 ○ 2 ○ 3 ○ 4 ● 5 ○ 6
○ 7 ○ 8 ○ 9

* I don't anger easily. **(impulse control)**
○ 1 ○ 2 ○ 3 ○ 4 ○ 5 ○ 6
○ 7 ○ 8 ● 9

* I can wait to buy the newest trend in clothes or technology. **(delayed gratification)**
○ 1 ○ 2 ● 3 ○ 4 ○ 5 ○ 6
○ 7 ○ 8 ○ 9

* I am aware of whatever feelings I am having at any given moment. **(emotional self-awareness)**
○ 1 ○ 2 ○ 3 ○ 4 ○ 5 ● 6
○ 7 ○ 8 ○ 9

* I can acknowledge, and be understanding, when my friend is upset. **(empathy)**
○ 1 ○ 2 ○ 3 ○ 4 ○ 5 ○ 6
○ 7 ○ 8 ● 9

CHAPTER 6: THE EMOTIONAL YOU: The Importance of Emotional Intelligence

* In general, I am a happy person who expects good things to happen. **(optimism)**
○ 1   ○ 2   ○ 3   ○ 4   ○ 5   ○ 6
● 7   ○ 8   ○ 9

* When I am in a situation and things are not working out, I can come up with an alternative solution. **(problem-solving)**
○ 1   ○ 2   ○ 3   ○ 4   ○ 5   ○ 6
● 7   ○ 8   ○ 9

* I know how to behave appropriately in different social situations. **(social competencies)**
○ 1   ○ 2   ○ 3   ○ 4   ○ 5   ○ 6
○ 7   ○ 8   ● 9

* Even though there are wars, poverty, bad economies, and global warming, I still believe the future will be brighter. **(capacity to hope)**
○ 1   ○ 2   ○ 3   ○ 4   ○ 5   ● 6
○ 7   ○ 8   ○ 9

PART II: Trials and Tribulations

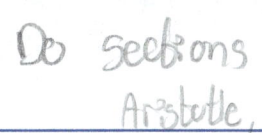

Daniel Goleman, Introduction "Aristotle's Challenge" and Chapter One "What Are Emotions For?"

Anyone can become angry—that is easy. But to be angry with the right person, to the right degree, at the right time, for the right purpose, and in the right way—this is not easy.

ARISTOTLE, *The Nicomachean Ethics*

It was an unbearably steamy August afternoon in New York City, the kind of sweaty day that makes people sullen with discomfort. I was heading back to a hotel, and as I stepped onto a bus up Madison Avenue I was startled by the driver, a middle-aged black man with an enthusiastic smile, who welcomed me with a friendly, "Hi! How you doing?" as I got on, a greeting he proffered to everyone else who entered as the bus wormed through the thick midtown traffic. Each passenger was as startled as I, and, locked into the morose mood of the day, few returned his greeting.

But as the bus crawled uptown through the gridlock, a slow, rather magical transformation occurred. The driver gave a running monologue for our benefit, a lively commentary on the passing scene around us: there was a terrific sale at that store, a wonderful exhibit at this museum, did you hear about the new movie that just opened at that cinema down the block? His delight in the rich possibilities the city offered was infectious. By the time people got off the bus, each in turn had shaken off the sullen-shell they had entered with, and when the driver shouted out a "So long, have a great day!" each gave a smiling response.

The memory of that encounter has stayed with me for close to twenty years. When I rode that Madison Avenue bus, I had just finished my own doctorate in psychology-but there was scant attention paid in the psychology of the day to just how such a transformation could happen. Psychological science knew little or nothing of the mechanics of emotion. And yet, imagining the spreading virus of good feeling that must have rippled through the city, starting from passengers on his bus, I saw that this bus driver was an urban peacemaker of sorts, wizardlike in his power to transmute the sullen irritability that seethed in his passengers, to soften and open their hearts a bit.

In stark contrast, some items from this week's paper:

- At a local school, a nine-year-old goes on a rampage, pouring paint over school desks, computers, and printers, and vandalizing a car in the school parking lot. The reason: some third-grade classmates called him a "baby" and he wanted to impress them.

- Eight youngsters are wounded when an inadvertent bump in a crowd of teenagers milling outside a Manhattan rap club leads to a shoving match, which ends when one of those affronted starts shooting a .38 caliber automatic handgun into the crowd. The report notes that such shootings over seemingly minor slights, which are perceived as acts of disrespect, have become increasingly common around the country in recent years.

- For murder victims under twelve, says a report, 57 percent of the murderers are their parents or stepparents. In almost half the cases, the parents say they were "merely trying to discipline the child." The

CHAPTER 6: THE EMOTIONAL YOU: The Importance of Emotional Intelligence

fatal beatings were prompted by "infractions" such as the child blocking the TV, crying, or soiling diapers.

- A German youth is on trial for murdering five Turkish women and girls in a fire he set while they slept. Part of a neo-Nazi group, he tells of failing to hold jobs, of drinking, of blaming his hard luck on foreigners. In a barely audible voice, he pleads, "I can't stop being sorry for what we've done, and I am infinitely ashamed."

Each day's news comes to us rife with such reports of the disintegration of civility and safety, an onslaught of mean-spirited impulse running amok. But the news simply reflects back to us on a larger scale a creeping sense of emotions out of control in our own lives and in those of the people around us. No one is insulated from this erratic ride of outburst and regret; it reaches into all of our lives in one way or another.

The last decade has seen a steady drumroll of reports like these, portraying an uptick in emotional ineptitude, desperation, and recklessness in our families, our communities, and our collective lives. These years have chronicled surging rage and despair, whether in the quiet loneliness of latchkey kids left with a TV for a babysitter, or in the pain of children abandoned, neglected, or abused, or in the ugly intimacy of marital violence. A spreading emotional malaise can be read in numbers showing a jump in depression around the world, and in the reminders of a surging tide of aggression—teens with guns in schools, freeway mishaps ending in shootings, disgruntled ex-employees massacring former fellow workers. *Emotional abuse, drive-by shooting,* and *post-traumatic stress* all entered the common lexicon over the last decade, as the slogan of the hour shifted from the cheery "Have a nice day" to the testiness of "Make my day."

This book is a guide to making sense of the senselessness. As a psychologist, and for the last decade as a journalist for *The New York Times,* I have I been tracking the progress of our scientific understanding of the realm of the irrational. From that perch I have been struck by two opposing trends, one portraying a growing calamity in our shared emotional life, the other offering some hopeful remedies.

WHY THIS EXPLORATION NOW

The last decade, despite its bad news, has also seen an unparalleled burst of scientific studies of emotion. Most dramatic are the glimpses of the brain at work, made possible by innovative methods such as new brain-imaging technologies. They have made visible for the first time in human history what has always been a source of deep mystery: exactly how this intricate mass of cells operates while we think and feel, imagine and dream. This flood of neurobiological data lets us understand more clearly than ever how the brain's centers for emotion move us to rage or to tears, and how more ancient parts of the brain, which stir us to make war as well as love, are channeled for better or worse. This unprecedented clarity on the workings of emotions and their failings brings into focus some fresh remedies for our collective emotional crisis.

I have had to wait till now before the scientific harvest was full enough to write this book. These insights are so late in coming largely because the place of feeling in mental life has been surprisingly slighted by research over the years, leaving the emotions a largely unexplored continent for scientific psychology. Into this void has rushed a welter of self-help books, well-intentioned advice based at best on clinical opinion but lacking much, if any, scientific basis. Now science is finally able to speak with authority to these urgent and perplexing questions of the psyche at its most irrational, to map with some precision the human heart.

This mapping offers a challenge to those who subscribe to a narrow view of intelligence, arguing that IQ is a genetic given that cannot be changed by life experience, and that our destiny in life is largely fixed by these aptitudes. That argument ignores the more challenging question: What can we change that will help our children fare better in life? What factors are at play, for example, when people of high IQ flounder and those of modest IQ do surprisingly well? I would argue that the difference quite often lies in the abilities called here *emotional intelligence,* which include self-control, zeal and persistence, and the ability to motivate oneself. And these skills, as we shall see, can be taught to children, giving them a better chance to use whatever intellectual potential the genetic lottery may have given them.

Beyond this possibility looms a pressing moral imperative. These are times when the fabric of society seems to unravel at ever-greater speed, when selfishness, violence, and a meanness of spirit seem to be rotting the goodness of our communal lives. Here the argument for the importance of emotional intelligence hinges on the link between sentiment, character, and moral instincts. There is growing evidence that fundamental ethical stances in life stem from underlying emotional capacities. For one, impulse is the medium of emotion; the seed of all impulse is a feeling bursting to express itself in action. Those who are at the mercy of impulse—who lack self-control—suffer a moral deficiency: The ability to control impulse is the base of will and character. By the same token, the root of altruism lies in empathy, the ability to read emotions in others; lacking a sense of another's need or despair, there is no caring. And if there are any two moral stances that our times call for, they are precisely these, self-restraint and compassion.

OUR JOURNEY

In this book I serve as a guide in a journey through these scientific insights into the emotions, a voyage aimed at bringing greater understanding to some of the most perplexing moments in our own lives and in the world around us. The journey's end is to understand what it means-and how-to bring intelligence to emotion. This understanding itself can help to some degree; bringing cognizance to the realm of feeling has an effect something like the impact of an observer at the quantum level in physics, altering what is being observed.

Our journey begins in Part One with new discoveries about the brain's emotional architecture that offer an explanation of those most baffling moments in our lives when feeling overwhelms all rationality. Understanding the interplay of brain structures that rule our moments of rage and fear- or passion and joy-reveals much about how we learn the emotional habits that can undermine our best intentions, as well as what we can do to subdue our more destructive or self-defeating emotional impulses. Most important, the neurological data suggest a window of opportunity for shaping our children's emotional habits.

The next major stop on our journey, Part Two of this book, is in seeing how neurological givens play out in the basic flair for living called *emotional intelligence:* being able, for example, to rein in emotional impulse; to read another's innermost feelings; to handle relationships smoothly-as Aristotle put it, the rare skill "to be angry with the right person, to the right degree, at the right time, for the right purpose, and in the right way." (Readers who are not drawn to neurological detail may want to proceed directly to this section.)

This expanded model of what it means to be "intelligent" puts emotions at the center of aptitudes for living. Part Three examines some key differences this aptitude makes: how these abilities can preserve our most prized relationships, or their lack corrode them; how the market forces that are reshaping our worklife are putting an unprecedented premium on emotional intelligence for on-the-job success; and how toxic emotions put our physical health at as much risk as does chain-smoking, even as emotional balance can help protect our health and well-being.

Our genetic heritage endows each of us with a series of emotional setpoints that determines our temperament. But the brain circuitry involved is extraordinarily malleable; temperament is not destiny. As Part Four shows, the emotional lessons we learn as children at home and at school shape the emotional circuits, making us more adept-or inept-at the basics of emotional intelligence. This means that childhood and adolescence are critical windows of opportunity for setting down the essential emotional habits that will govern our lives.

Part Five explores what hazards await those who, in growing to maturity, fail to master the emotional realm-how deficiencies in emotional intelligence heighten a spectrum of risks, from depression or a life of violence to eating disorders and drug abuse. And it documents how pioneering schools are teaching children the emotional and social skills they need to keep their lives on track.

Perhaps the most disturbing single piece of data in this book comes from a massive survey of parents and teachers and shows a worldwide trend for the present generation of children to be more troubled emotionally than the last: more lonely and depressed, more angry and unruly, more nervous and prone to worry, more impulsive and aggressive.

If there is a remedy, I feel it must lie in how we prepare our young for life. At present we leave the emotional education of our children to chance, with ever more disastrous results. One solution is a new vision of what schools can do to educate the whole student, bringing together mind and heart in the classroom. Our journey ends with visits to innovative classes that aim to give children a grounding in the basics of emotional intelligence. I can foresee a day when education will routinely include inculcating essential human competencies such as self-awareness, self-control, and empathy, and the arts of listening, resolving conflicts, and cooperation.

In *The Nicomachean Ethics*, Aristotle's philosophical enquiry into virtue, character, and the good life, his challenge is to manage our emotional life with intelligence. Our passions, when well exercised, have wisdom; they guide our thinking, our values, our survival. But they can easily go awry, and do so all too often. As Aristotle saw, the problem is not with emotionality, but with the *appropriateness* of emotion and its expression. The question is, how can we bring intelligence to our emotions-and civility to our streets and caring to our communal life?

PART ONE
The Emotional Brain

What Are Emotions For?
It is with the heart that one sees rightly; what is essential is invisible to the eye.

ANTOINE DE SAINT-EXUPÉRY,
The Little Prince

Ponder the last moments of Gary and Mary Jane Chauncey, a couple completely devoted to their eleven-year-old daughter Andrea, who was confined to a wheelchair by cerebral palsy. The Chauncey family were passengers on an Amtrak train that crashed into a river after a barge hit and weakened a railroad bridge in Louisiana's bayou country. Thinking first of their daughter, the couple tried their best to save Andrea as water rushed into the sinking train; somehow they managed to push Andrea through a window to rescuers. Then, as the car sank beneath the water, they perished.

Andrea's story, of parents whose last heroic act is to ensure their child's survival, captures a moment of almost mythic courage. Without doubt such incidents of parental sacrifice for their progeny have been repeated countless times in human history and prehistory, and countless more in the larger course of evolution of our species. Seen from the perspective of evolutionary biologists, such parental self-sacrifice is in the service of "reproductive success" in passing on one's genes to future generations. But from the perspective of a parent making a desperate decision in a moment of crisis, it is about nothing other than love.

As an insight into the purpose and potency of emotions, this exemplary act of parental heroism testifies to the role of altruistic love-and every other emotion we feel—in human life.[3] It suggests that our deepest feelings, our passions and longings, are essential guides, and that our species owes much of its existence to their power in human affairs. That power is extraordinary: Only a potent love—the urgency of saving a cherished child—could lead a parent to override the impulse for personal survival. Seen from the intellect, their self-sacrifice was arguably irrational; seen from the heart, it was the only choice to make.

Sociobiologists point to the preeminence of heart over head at such crucial moments when they conjecture about why evolution has given emotion such a central role in the human psyche. Our emotions, they say, guide us in facing predicaments and tasks too important to leave to intellect alone-danger, painful loss, persisting toward a goal despite frustrations, bonding with a mate, building a family. Each emotion offers a distinctive readiness to act, each points us in a direction that has worked well to handle the recurring challenges of human life. As these eternal situations were repeated and repeated over our evolutionary history, the survival value of our emotional repertoire was attested to by its becoming imprinted in our nerves as innate, automatic tendencies of the human heart.

A view of human nature that ignores the power of emotions is sadly shortsighted. The very name Homo *sapiens,* the thinking species, is misleading in light of the new appreciation and vision of the place of emotions in our lives that science now offers. As we all know from experience, when it comes to shaping our decisions and our actions, feeling counts every bit as much—and often more—than thought. We have gone too far in emphasizing the value and import of the purely rational—of what IQ measures in human life. For better or worse, intelligence can come to nothing when the emotions hold sway.

WHEN PASSIONS OVERWHELM REASON

It was a tragedy of errors. Fourteen-year-old Matilda Crabtree was just playing a practical joke on her father: she jumped out of a closet and yelled "Boo!" as her parents came home at one in the morning from visiting friends.

But Bobby Crabtree and his wife thought Matilda was staying with friends that night. Hearing noises as he entered the house, Crabtree reached for his .357 caliber pistol and went into Matilda's bedroom to investigate. When his daughter jumped from the closet. Crabtree shot her in the neck. Matilda Crabtree died twelve hours later.

One emotional legacy of evolution is the fear that mobilizes us to protect our family from danger; that impulse impelled Bobby Crabtree to get his gun and search his house for the intruder he thought was prowling there. Fear primed Crabtree to shoot before he could fully register what he was shooting at, even before he could recognize his daughter's voice. Automatic reactions of this sort have become etched in our nervous system, evolutionary biologists presume, because for a long and crucial period in human prehistory they made the difference between survival and death. Even more important, they mattered for the main task of evolution: being able to bear progeny who would carry on these very genetic predispositions—a sad irony, given the tragedy at the Crabtree household.

But while our emotions have been wise guides in the evolutionary long run, the new realities civilization presents have arisen with such rapidity that the slow march of evolution cannot keep up. Indeed, the first laws and proclamations of ethics—the Code of Hammurabi, the Ten Commandments of the Hebrews, the Edicts of Emperor Ashoka—can be read as attempts to harness, subdue, and domesticate emotional life. As Freud described in *Civilization and Its Discontents*, society has had to enforce from without rules meant to subdue tides of emotional excess that surge too freely within.

Despite these social constraints, passions overwhelm reason time and again. This given of human nature arises from the basic architecture of mental life. In terms of biological design for the basic neural circuitry of emotion, what we are born with is what worked best for the last 50,000 human generations, not the last 500 generations—and certainly not the last five. The slow, deliberate forces of evolution that have shaped our emotions have done their work over the course of a million years; the last 10,000 years-despite having witnessed the rapid rise of human civilization and the explosion of the human population from five million to five billion-have left little imprint on our biological templates for emotional life.

For better or for worse, our appraisal of every personal encounter and our responses to it are shaped not just by our rational judgments or our personal history, but also by our distant ancestral past. This leaves us with sometimes tragic propensities, as witness the sad events at the Crabtree household. In short, we too often confront postmodern dilemmas with an emotional repertoire tailored to the urgencies of the Pleistocene. That predicament is at the heart of my subject.

Impulses to Action

One early spring day I was driving along a highway over a mountain pass in Colorado, when a snow flurry suddenly blotted out the car a few lengths ahead of me. As I peered ahead I couldn't make out anything; the swirling snow was now a blinding whiteness. Pressing my foot on the brake, I could feel anxiety flood my body and hear the thumping of my heart.

The anxiety built to full fear: I pulled over to the side of the road, waiting for the flurry to pass. A half hour later the snow stopped, visibility returned, and I continued on my way—only to be stopped a few hundred yards down the road, where an ambulance crew was helping a passenger in a car that had rear-ended a slower car in front; the collision blocked the highway. If I had continued driving in the blinding snow, I probably would have hit them.

The caution fear forced on me that day may have saved my life. Like a rabbit frozen in terror at the hint of a passing fox— or a protomammal hiding from a marauding dinosaur-I was overtaken by an internal state that compelled me to stop, pay attention, and take heed of a coming danger.

PART II: Trials and Tribulations

All emotions are, in essence, impulses to act, the instant plans for handling life that evolution has instilled in us. The very root of the word *emotion is motere,* the Latin verb "to move," plus the prefix "e-" to connote "move away," suggesting that a tendency to act is implicit in every emotion. That emotions lead to actions is most obvious in watching animals or children; it is only in "civilized" adults we so often find the great anomaly in the animal kingdom, emotions-root impulses to act-divorced from obvious reaction.

In our emotional repertoire each emotion plays a unique role, as revealed by their distinctive biological signatures (see Appendix A for details on "basic" emotions). With new methods to peer into the body and brain, researchers are discovering more physiological details of how each emotion prepares the body for a very different kind of response:

- With *anger* blood flows to the hands, making it easier to grasp a weapon or strike at a foe; heart rate increases, and a rush of hormones such as adrenaline generates a pulse of energy strong enough for vigorous action.

- With *fear* blood goes to the large skeletal muscles, such as in the legs, making it easier to flee-and making the face blanch as blood is shunted away from it (creating the feeling that the blood "runs cold"). At the same time, the body freezes, if only for a moment, perhaps allowing time to gauge whether hiding might be a better reaction. Circuits in the brain's emotional centers trigger a flood of hormones that put the body on general alert, making it edgy and ready for action, and attention fixates on the threat at hand, the better to evaluate what response to make.

- Among the main biological changes in *happiness* is an increased activity in a brain center that inhibits negative feelings and fosters an increase in available energy, and a quieting of those that generate worrisome thought. But there is no particular shift in physiology save a quiescence, which makes the body recover more quickly from the biological arousal of upsetting emotions. This configuration offers the body a general rest, as well as readiness and enthusiasm for whatever task is at hand and for striving toward a great variety of goals.

- *Love*, tender feelings, and sexual satisfaction entail parasympathetic arousal-the physiological opposite of the "fight-or-flight" mobilization shared by fear and anger. The parasympathetic pattern, dubbed the "relaxation response," is a bodywide set of reactions that generates a general state of calm and contentment, facilitating cooperation.

- The lifting of the eyebrows in *surprise* allows the taking in of a larger visual sweep and also permits more light to strike the retina. This offers more information about the unexpected event, making it easier to figure out exactly what is going on and concoct the best plan for action.

- Around the world an expression of *disgust* looks the same, and sends the identical message: something is offensive in taste or smell, or metaphorically so. The facial expression of disgust-the upper lip curled to the side as the nose wrinkles slightly-suggests a primordial attempt, as Darwin observed, to close the nostrils against a noxious odor or to spit out a poisonous food.

- A main function for *sadness* is to help adjust to a significant loss, such as the death of someone close

CHAPTER 6: THE EMOTIONAL YOU: The Importance of Emotional Intelligence

or a major disappointment. Sadness brings a drop in energy and enthusiasm for life's activities, particularly diversions and pleasures, and, as it deepens and approaches depression, slows the body's metabolism. This introspective withdrawal creates the opportunity to mourn a loss or frustrated hope, grasp its consequences for one's life, and, as energy returns, plan new beginnings. This loss of energy may well have kept saddened-and vulnerable-early humans close to home, where they were safer.

These biological propensities to act are shaped further by our life experience and our culture. For instance, universally the loss of a loved one elicits sadness and grief. But how we show our grieving-how emotions are displayed or held back for private moments-is molded by culture, as are which particular people in our lives fall into the category of "loved ones" to be mourned.

The protracted period of evolution when these emotional responses were hammered into shape was certainly a harsher reality than most humans endured as a species after the dawn of recorded history. It was a time when few infants survived to childhood and few adults to thirty years, when predators could strike at any moment, when the vagaries of droughts and floods meant the difference between starvation and survival. But with the coming of agriculture and even the most rudimentary human societies, the odds for survival began to change dramatically. In the last ten thousand years, when these advances took hold throughout the world, the ferocious pressures that had held the human population in check eased steadily.

Those same pressures had made our emotional responses so valuable for survival; as they waned, so did the goodness of fit of parts of our emotional repertoire. While in the ancient past a hair-trigger anger may have offered a crucial edge for survival, the availability of automatic weaponry to thirteen year- olds has made it too often a disastrous reaction.

Our Two Minds

A friend was telling me about her divorce, a painful separation. Her husband had fallen in love with a younger woman at work, and suddenly announced he was leaving to live with the other woman. Months of bitter wrangling over house, money, and custody of the children followed. Now, some months later, she was saying that her independence was appealing to her, that she was happy to be on her own. "I just don't think about him anymore—I really don't care," she said. But as she said it, her eyes momentarily welled up with tears.

That moment of teary eyes could easily pass unnoted. But the empathic understanding that someone's watering eyes means she is sad despite her words to the contrary is an act of comprehending just as surely as is distilling meaning from words on a printed page. One is an act of the emotional mind, the other of the rational mind. In a very real sense we have two minds, one that thinks and one that feels.

These two fundamentally different ways of knowing interact to construct our mental life. One, the rational mind, is the mode of comprehension we are typically conscious of: more prominent in awareness, thoughtful, able to ponder and reflect. But alongside that there is another system of knowing: impulsive and powerful, if sometimes illogical-the emotional mind. (For a more detailed description of the characteristics of the emotional mind, see Appendix B.)

The emotional/rational dichotomy approximates the folk distinction between "heart" and "head"; knowing something is right "in your heart" is a different order of conviction-somehow a deeper kind of certainty-than thinking so with your rational mind. There is a steady gradient in the ratio of rational-to-emotional control over the mind; the more intense the feeling, the more dominant the emotional mind becomes—and the more ineffectual, the rational. This is an arrangement that seems to stem from eons of evolutionary advantage to having emotions and intuitions guide our instantaneous response in situations where our lives are in peril—and where pausing to think over what to do could cost us our lives.

These two minds, the emotional and the rational, operate in tight harmony for the most part, intertwining their very different ways of knowing to guide us through the world. Ordinarily there is a balance between emotional and rational minds, with emotion feeding into and informing the operations of the rational mind, and the rational mind refining and sometimes vetoing the inputs of the emotions. Still, the emotional and rational minds are semi-independent faculties, each, as we shall see, reflecting the operation of distinct, but interconnected, circuitry in the brain.

In many or most moments these minds are exquisitely coordinated; feelings are essential to thought, thought to feeling. But when passions surge the balance tips: it is the emotional mind that captures the upper hand, swamping the rational mind. The sixteenth-century humanist Erasmus of Rotterdam wrote in a satirical vein of this perennial tension between reason and emotion

> Jupiter has bestowed far more passion than reason-you could calculate the ratio as 24 to one. He set up two raging tyrants in opposition to Reason's solitary power: anger and lust. How far Reason can prevail against the combined forces of these two the common life of man makes quite clear. Reason does the only thing she can and shouts herself hoarse, repeating formulas of virtue, while the other two bid her go hang herself, and are increasingly noisy and offensive, until at last their Ruler is exhausted, gives up, and surrenders.

HOW THE BRAIN GREW

To better grasp the potent hold of the emotions on the thinking mind-and why feeling and reason are so readily at war-consider how the brain evolved. Human brains, with their three pounds or so of cells and neural juices, are about triple the size of those in our nearest cousins in evolution, the nonhuman primates. Over millions of years of evolution, the brain has grown from the bottom up, with its higher centers developing as elaborations of lower, more ancient parts. (The growth of the brain in the human embryo roughly retraces this evolutionary course.)

The most primitive part of the brain, shared with all species that have more than a minimal nervous system, is the brainstem surrounding the top of the spinal cord. This root brain regulates basic life functions like breathing and the metabolism of the body's other organs, as well as controlling stereotyped reactions and movements. This primitive brain cannot be said to think or learn; rather it is a set of preprogrammed regulators that keep the body running as it should and reacting in a way that ensures survival. This brain reigned supreme in the Age of the Reptiles: Picture a snake hissing to signal the threat of an attack.

From the most primitive root, the brainstem, emerged the emotional centers. Millions of years later in evolution, from these emotional areas evolved the thinking brain or "neocortex." the giant bulb of convoluted tissues that make up the top layers. The fact that the thinking brain grew from the emotional reveals much about the relationship of thought to feeling; there was an emotional brain long before there was a rational one.

The most ancient root of our emotional life is in the sense of smell, or, more precisely, in the olfactory lobe, the cells that take in and analyze smell. Every living entity, be it nutritious, poisonous, sexual partner, predator or prey, has a distinctive molecular signature that can be carried in the wind. In those primitive times smell commended itself as a paramount sense for survival.

From the olfactory lobe the ancient centers for emotion began to evolve, eventually growing large enough to encircle the top of the brainstem. In its rudimentary stages, the olfactory center was composed of little more than thin layers of neurons gathered to analyze smell. One layer of cells took in what was smelled and sorted it out into the relevant categories: edible or toxic, sexually available, enemy or meal. A second layer of cells sent reflexive messages throughout the nervous system telling the body what to do: bite, spit, approach, flee, chase.

With the arrival of the first mammals came new, key layers of the emotional brain. These, surrounding the brainstem, look roughly like a bagel with a bite taken out at the bottom where the brainstem nestles into them. Because this part of the brain rings and borders the brainstem, it was called the "limbic" system, from "limbus," the Latin word for "ring." This new neural territory added emotions proper to the brain's repertoire. When we are in the grip of craving or fury, head-over-heels in love or recoiling in dread, it is the limbic system that has us in its grip.

As it evolved, the limbic system refined two powerful tools: learning and memory. These revolutionary advances allowed an animal to be much smarter in its choices for survival, and to fine-tune its responses to adapt changing demands rather than having invariable and automatic reactions. If a food led to sickness, it could be avoided next time. Decisions like knowing what to spurn were still determined largely through smell; the connections between the olfactory bulb and the limbic system now took on the tasks of making distinctions among smells and recognizing them, comparing a present smell and with past ones, and so discriminating good from bad. This was done by the "rhinencephalon," literally, the "nose brain," a part of the limbic wiring, and the rudimentary basis of the neocortex, the thinking brain.

About 100 million years ago, the brain in mammals took a great growth spurt. Piled on top of the thin two-layered cortex—the regions that plan, comprehend what is sensed, coordinate movement—several new layers of brain cells were added to form the neocortex. In contrast to the ancient brain's two-layered cortex, the neocortex offered an extraordinary intellectual edge.

The *Homo sapiens* neocortex, so much larger than in any other species, has added all that is distinctly human. The neocortex is the seat of thought; it contains the centers that put together and comprehend what the senses perceive. It adds to a feeling what we think about it—and allows us to have feelings about ideas, art, symbols and imaginings.

In evolution the neocortex allowed a judicious fine-tuning that no doubt has made enormous advantages in an organism's ability to survive adversity, making it more likely that its progeny would in turn pass on the genes that contain the same neural circuitry. The survival edge is due to the neocortex's talent for strategizing, long-term planning, and other mental wiles. Beyond that, the triumphs of art, of civilization and culture, are all fruits of the neocortex.

This new addition to the brain allowed the addition of nuance to emotional life. Take love. Limbic structures generate feelings of pleasure and sexual desire—the emotions that feed sexual passion. But the addition of the neocortex and its connections to the limbic system allowed for the mother-child bond that is the basis of the family unit and the long-term commitment to childrearing that makes human development possible. (Species that that have no neocortex, such as reptiles, lack maternal affection; when their young hatch, the newborns must hide to avoid being cannibalized.) In humans the protective bond between parent and child allows much of maturation to go on over the course of a long childhood—during which the brain continues to develop.

As we proceed up the phylogenic scale from reptile to rhesus to human, the sheer mass of the neocortex increases; with that increase comes a geometric rise in the interconnections in brain circuitry. The larger the number of such connections, the greater the range of possible responses. The neocortex allows for the subtlety and complexity of emotional life, such as the ability to have feelings about our feelings. There is more neocortex-to-limbic system in primates than in other species—and vastly more in humans—suggesting why we are able to display a far greater range of reactions to our emotions, and more nuance. While a rabbit or rhesus has a restricted set of typical responses to fear, the larger human neocortex allows a far more nimble repertoire—including calling 911. The more complex the social system, the more essential is such flexibility-and there is no more complex social world than our own.

But these higher centers do not govern all of emotional life; in crucial matters of the heart-and most especially in emotional emergencies-they can be said to defer to the limbic system. Because so many of the brain's higher centers sprouted from or extended the scope of the limbic area, the emotional brain plays a crucial role in neural architecture. As the root from which the newer brain grew, the emotional areas are intertwined via myriad connecting circuits to all parts of the neocortex. This gives the emotional centers immense power to influence the functioning of the rest of the brain including its centers for thought.

Excerpts from "Emotional Intelligence" by Daniel Goleman, Copyright © 1995 by Daniel Goleman. Used by permission of Bantam Books, an imprint of Random House, a division of Random House, LLC. All rights reserved.

Reflective FOCUS

▼   What is your emotional addiction?

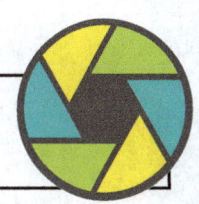

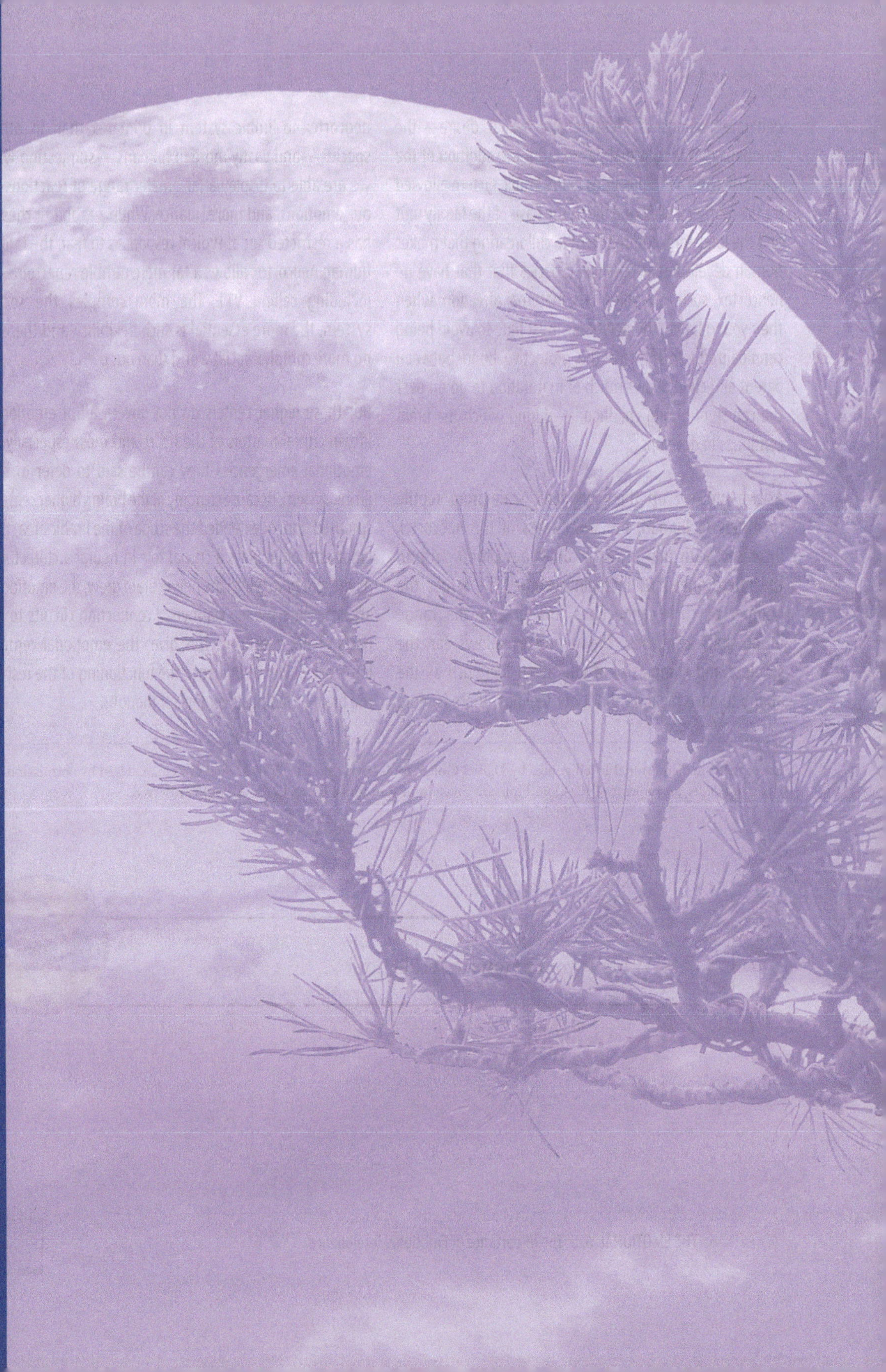

chapter 7

The Social You

SOCIAL INTELLIGENCE AND DIVERSITY

Image © Andrey_Popov, 2014. Used under license from Shutterstock, Inc.

You cannot hope to build a better world without improving individuals. To that end each of us must work for our own improvement and at the same time share a general responsibility for all humanity...

–Marie Curie (1867–1934)

Advances in technology have brought us global use of the Internet, smartphones, and instant messaging. From preschoolers to grandmothers, from Orlando to Shanghai, almost everyone has a cell phone stuck to their ear or at their fingertips. You only have to walk down a New York City street during lunch hour to hear the cacophony of voices as people talk on their cell phones while rushing to their destinations. And then, there are those whose favorite mode of communication is to text message in truncated words or send endless e-mail messages. No human contact for them. The common denominator is that as people engage with technology, they become increasingly oblivious to those around them, and often find it difficult to communicate face to face with other people and to interact in a socially appropriate manner.

Social etiquette and civility are quickly becoming a things of the past. How many times have you gone out to dinner with friends and once seated, everyone pulls out their smartphone and lays it next to the knife or fork as though it is another utensil. You begin a conversation with your friend and you notice even as she is listening to you, she has one eye on the phone to see if she has a text coming through. If the phone buzzes or lights up that is the end of the conversation. Nothing is as important as whoever is on the phone.

With the increased use of cell phones and social media sites like Twitter, Facebook. Instagram, YouTube, and Tumblr, to name but a few, we have seen the birth of cyber bullying, sexting, shaming, and internet addiction to gaming and social media.

Internet gaming addiction is now listed as a mental illness in the Diagnostic and Statistical Manual of Mental Disorders – DSM-5. The inclusion of internet gaming addiction in the DSM 5 is partly based on the national health crisis that some Asian countries are experiencing as a result of large numbers of their youth participating in internet gaming, social media, and virtual realities to such an extent that the behavior is isolating them from society. When brain scans are done on individuals who are addicted to the internet, changes are seen in their brains that resemble patterns in alcoholics and drug users.

Technology is going to continue to develop in new ways that will impact us both positively and negatively. And it is for this reason, that it is so important to understand and develop social intelligence.

Social Competencies

Although global communication technology gives us the freedom to communicate worldwide, it can also isolate us from human contact. As a consequence of isolation, our social *competencies* become rusty or underdeveloped.

In the previous section, we discussed the concept of emotional intelligence and the importance of managing your emotions to support your success. One of the characteristics of emotional intelligence mentioned was **social competencies**, which can be viewed as an aspect of social intelligence. Emotional intelligence is the **internal** self-awareness and self-management of emotions, whereas social intelligence can be seen as **externally** oriented competencies and awareness of emotions. You need to be skilled in both to be successful.

The term "social intelligence" was first coined by E.L. Thorndike in an article in *Harper's Weekly* magazine in 1920. According to Thorndike, the term "social intelligence" was a person's ability to understand and manage other people, and to engage in appropriate social interactions.

Most recently, the concept of social intelligence has been explored by Daniel Goleman in his book, *Social Intelligence: The Revolutionary New Science of Human Relationships*. Goleman hypothesizes that social intelligence is a **function of both cognition and biology** (brain based), and it is comprised of two categories: **social awareness** and **social facility**. Earlier theorists posited that social intelligence was primarily related to cognition or the thinking/learning process. This section will focus on Goleman's interpretation of social intelligence and its origins.

Social Awareness

In the social intelligence context, social awareness has to do with what we sense about others. The mechanisms that assist us in "reading" social situations or people are primal empathy, attunement, empathetic accuracy, and social cognition.

Primal empathy is the ability to pick up cues from another person's expressions. When triggered by gut-level empathy, "mirror neurons" in the brain operate rapidly and automatically in picking up these cues. For example, Janey is a bank teller. A customer comes to her station. Janey looks at the customer's face and senses something strange about the customer. A fleeting tense look crosses the customer's face. Janey pushes the panic button as the customer pulls out a gun. This is the brain's intuitive, rapid, and spontaneous assessment of the non-verbal cues.

Attunement is the ability to give a person you are speaking with your undivided attention, by being fully present in the moment, and using "active" listening skills. Active listening, also known as **focused listening**, is being attuned to the other person's feelings and allowing for verbal give-and-take in the conversation.

Often, we spend so much time multitasking that we are not really listening to the other person. Tom is in his office working on the computer. Mary comes in to talk. Tom is listening to Mary, but his eyes dart back and forth from Mary's face to the computer screen, and then to the cell phone lying open on his desk. Tom is not exhibiting attunement.

Empathetic accuracy is the ability to "read" another person accurately—that is, to have an **actual understanding** of what the other person feels or thinks. It is having an awareness of another's intentions and being correct in your perceptions.

FIGURE 7.1: Focused listening

In the brain, empathetic accuracy utilizes the neocortex (thinking part of the brain), especially the prefrontal lobes (mirror neurons). The mirror neurons help us to subliminally access what a person intends to do through picking up nonverbal cues in facial expressions, body language, and energy; and the neocortex makes it conscious and validates the subliminal information.

Social cognition is the ability to perceive the world as it really is, and not as you would like it to be. People who have this ability are able to discern what is expected in terms of behavior, and appropriateness in almost any social situation. This ability involves having strong interpersonal knowledge, and a kind of social savvy that allows a person to "read" social situations and the people in those social settings.

Social Facility

According to Goleman, the second category of social intelligence is **social facility**. *Social facility evolves out of social awareness to create smooth, effective interactions.* Social facility includes synchrony, self-presentation, influence, and concern.

Synchrony involves the ability to read the nonverbal cues of another person. The mirror neurons play an important part in synchrony. Our capacity to immediately discern the nonverbal cues, and act on them without thinking, resides in this neural network of mirror neurons. Synchrony is operating when you nod your head in response to something another is saying, or when your body positions mirror the body positions of the person with whom you are having a conversation.

Self-presentation is the capacity to project confidence and personality regardless of one's underlying emotional state. Self-presentation communicates to others what you think about yourself through your appearance, mood, demeanor, body language, and how you occupy space in a room. Do you walk into a room as if you own it, or do you shrink to be unobtrusive and stay in the perimeter of a room?

Self-presentation is the skill that allows you to control and mask your emotional expressions in social situations where expressing your feelings may be inappropriate. Professor Jones, for example, is to be the keynote speaker at a conference on global warming. The night before the conference, Professor Jones's beloved dog suddenly passes away. Professor Jones is grief stricken. She cries every time she thinks of her dog. She would like to cancel the speech, but she has made a commitment to appear at the conference. The next morning, Professor Jones puts on her "game face," gets her emotions under control, and proceeds to give the speech. The audience perceives her as professional, knowledgeable, charming, and funny.

Self-presentation is about showing yourself in the best possible light. Are you viewed as approachable? Do you convey a sense of confidence, professionalism, warmth, kindness, friendliness, or do you project shyness, insecurity, and indifference? There is an old saying, "You never get a second chance to make a first impression."

Influence is the skill that enables a person, through his or her own efforts, to constructively shape the outcome of a situation. It is the ability to express yourself in a way that produces a result that you desire. Influence requires that you understand: (a) the cultural and social context of the situation you want to influence; (b) the intensity of expression you need to employ to influence the situation in your favor; and (c) that information needs to be presented clearly so that it is easily comprehended.

Concern is having compassion. *Compassion is empathy put into action.* Concern dictates that when you see a person in distress, you don't just say, "I know how you feel." Instead, you take the next step and say, "Is there anything I can do to help you move out of this distressed state?" Concern prods you to take responsibility for what needs to be done. If you have the capacity to show concern, you are more likely to help your colleagues, and to understand the need for teamwork.

Studies have found that individuals who are most physiologically aroused by seeing a person in distress (i.e., they empathize, feel anxious or upset) are more likely to help that person. Individuals who show very little empathy toward a person in distress tend not to offer assistance.

Low Road and High Road

In his book, Goleman discusses the idea that the human brain, through its intricate and wide-ranging neural networks, is designed to be "social" and to assist us in relating to others. He calls the **brain-based aspects of social intelligence "low road"** aptitudes, such as primal empathy that is dependent on the activity of "mirror neurons" in the brain. He calls the aspects that **require cognition "high road"** aptitudes, such as influence that requires social awareness, knowledge, and social context. Although he identifies these as two ends of the spectrum, Goleman also cautions that "high road" social intelligence aptitudes also involve "low road" neural pathways, such as mirror neurons in the brain. Empathetic accuracy is an example of both a low-road and high-road ability. The mirror neurons activate to pick up the subtle signs of disturbance in an individual (primal empathy), but accurately interpreting what someone else feels, and thinks resides in the cognitive area of the brain (the neocortex).

Neuroscience research in social intelligence is relatively new, and has not yet precisely mapped out the areas that pertain to the "social brain." At this juncture, it is difficult to say whether you can do things to enhance the "low road" aspects to improve social intelligence. Research is ongoing in this area and perhaps, at some time in the future, scientists will discover ways to enhance the functioning of these neurons.

However, it is likely that you can improve some of the "high road" or more cognitive aspects of social intelligence through self-monitoring, and conscious changes in behavior. What are the areas you could work on?

Ways to enhance your social intelligence skills
- Improve your listening skills.
- Develop a respectful interest in others.
- Learn to read the context (meaning) in a situation.
- Observe people to see how they relate to "space."
- Pay attention to body language cues/nonverbal communication.
- Assess how you present yourself to the world.
- Make appropriate changes to enhance your self-presentation.

- Educate yourself about diverse cultures, their customs, and social expectations.
- Learn about the "culture" of the groups to which you belong (family, coworkers, students, religious groups).
- Study how the social world really works.
- Learn how to behave according to the rules of your social setting.
- Find a role model who displays social intelligence abilities.

FOCUS AND SUCCESS

In his latest book entitled Focus: The Hidden Driver of Success, Daniel Goleman takes social intelligence a step further by exploring the concept of "focus." For Goleman, focus is the ability of an individual to direct their attention or effort to something specific without allowing distraction to interfere with their attention.

Goleman says there are three kinds of focus: inner focus, outer focus, and systems focus. Inner focus has to do with self-understanding, intuition, inner guidance, and personal values. Outer focus which encompasses the aspects of social awareness (empathy, communication, interpersonal skills). And system focus which utilizes the social intelligence skill of social cognition or the ability to see the larger world as it is and to "read" situations as they occur.

Why is it important to have the ability to focus? The world around us is filled with distractions and stimuli as are the individual lives we lead. The brain is constantly processing what we see, feel and hear almost, at times, to overload capacity. The ability to zone in on one area while dismissing other incoming stimuli allows us to make better plans, decisions, and choices.

How can you improve your ability to focus? Just like exercising to build a muscle, the brain needs to practice to develop its ability to focus. Some of the ways to help develop your attention or focus are: meditation, mindfulness, memorization, and concentration.

FIGURE 7.2: Focus

CHAPTER 7: THE SOCIAL YOU: Social Intelligence and Diversity

Meditation teaches the brain to release distracting thoughts while paying attention to the breath. There are different types of meditation you can practice and they all help to enhance your ability to focus.

Mindfulness is the practice of paying attention to whatever you are doing at a given. One example of how mindfulness can be practiced is in the process of eating a meal. Before sitting down to eat you turn off the television or radio and put away any reading materials. You now can concentrate solely on eating your food. You observe the smell, the look, and feel of your food before tasting it. Once the food is in your mouth you chew slowly before swallowing. The repeated practice of mindful eating will increase your capacity to focus in other areas of your life

Memorization is the practice of remembering. To improve your memory try reading a poem then reciting it a loud without looking at the text.

Concentration is developed by focusing your attention without distraction for a period of time. A quick exercise you can do is to stare at your thumbnail for a minute without letting other things in the environment move your attention away from the thumbnail.

Innovation, ingenuity, and creativity come from an individual's capacity to turn inward, quiet the mind, and and focus.

Social Intelligence and You

On the hero's journey, you face many trials and tribulations that can steer you off course as you follow your path to bliss. We have already discussed the ways in which meaning of life, needs, locus of control, self-esteem, and emotional intelligence can make your journey easier or more difficult. We can add social intelligence to this list as a potential obstacle or asset.

Social intelligence is about your ability to interact with the external environment in effective ways. It impacts all of your relationships: family, friends, fellow students, coworkers, supervisors. The more evolved your social intelligence, the better your relationships and your experiences in the social world will be.

Marry your social intelligence skills with your ability to focus your attention like a laser and the possibilities for you will be endless.

Social Intelligence Assessment

Find out you how rate on this Social Intelligence Assessment

Rate yourself in each ability on a scale of 1–9. 1–3 = low ability; 4–6 = average ability; 7–9 = high ability

* Interested in the world at large and see the world realistically. **(social cognition)**
    - ○ 1
    - ○ 2
    - ○ 3
    - ○ 4
    - ○ 5
    - ○ 6
    - ○ 7
    - ○ 8
    - ○ 9

* Have the ability to understand the rules of society and to behave accordingly. **(social cognition)**
    - ○ 1
    - ○ 2
    - ○ 3
    - ○ 4
    - ○ 5
    - ○ 6
    - ○ 7
    - ○ 8
    - ○ 9

* Have the ability to be sensitive to other people's needs and desires. **(concern)**
    - ○ 1
    - ○ 2
    - ○ 3
    - ○ 4
    - ○ 5
    - ○ 6
    - ○ 7
    - ○ 8
    - ○ 9

* Have the ability to "read" situations and to interpret the behaviors, intentions, and emotional states of people in those situations. **(primal accuracy)**
    - ○ 1
    - ○ 2
    - ○ 3
    - ○ 4
    - ○ 5
    - ○ 6
    - ○ 7
    - ○ 8
    - ○ 9

* Have the ability to adapt with ease to new social situations. **(social facility)**
    - ○ 1
    - ○ 2
    - ○ 3
    - ○ 4
    - ○ 5
    - ○ 6
    - ○ 7
    - ○ 8
    - ○ 9

* Have the ability to connect with and influence people. **(influence)**
  - ○ 1   ○ 2   ○ 3   ○ 4   ○ 5   ○ 6
  - ○ 7   ○ 8   ○ 9

* Have the ability to see the impact of your behavior on others. **(social awareness)**
  - ○ 1   ○ 2   ○ 3   ○ 4   ○ 5   ○ 6
  - ○ 7   ○ 8   ○ 9

* Have the ability to listen with focused attention as another person speaks. **(attunement)**
  - ○ 1   ○ 2   ○ 3   ○ 4   ○ 5   ○ 6
  - ○ 7   ○ 8   ○ 9

* Have the ability to be empathetic and compassionate. **(concern)**
  - ○ 1   ○ 2   ○ 3   ○ 4   ○ 5   ○ 6
  - ○ 7   ○ 8   ○ 9

Diversity

"No man is an island. No man stands alone entire of itself, every man is a piece of the continent, a part of the main."

John Donne wrote these words approximately 400 years ago, and the realization of this statement is more important than ever. Everyone lives and works in a world with others who are different in regard to personality, age, gender, race, religion, nationality, sexual preference, disability, or social class. Success in a career, and in life, depends heavily on one's knowledge, understanding, and ability to live in a diverse world.

Diversity, as an aspect of social intelligence, speaks to Maslow's second attribute "increased acceptance of self, of others and of nature—the individual will see human nature as it is, without judging themselves or others." Socially intelligent people understand that human beings are not meant to live in isolation. We are all interdependent and need to interact with each other in ways that are mutually accepting and empowering.

Connected and Disconnected

The world is intricately connected through economics, business, politics, families, and the most powerful connector of all, the Internet. As citizens of the planet, we are all affected by the same problems: the declining environment, AIDS/health crises, terrorism, immigration/emigration, poverty, and inequity. Although we are connected in all these ways, the world is increasingly disconnected because of disparities between modernized twenty-first-century countries and those countries that still follow traditional ways of the past.

The increase in population and decrease in resources on the planet create challenges on a global level. The major challenge is to discover ways to build a sustainable world through trade, technology, competition, freedom, prosperity, security, and preservation of natural resources and the environment.

Several changes in our collective thinking are required to meet the challenges of a changing and increasingly diverse world. We all need to feel and believe that we are citizens of the world, and not just our own countries. As citizens of the world, we become aware of issues

FIGURE 7.3: Diversity at "work"

both in our own country and abroad. Equally important is the understanding that we are all interdependent, interconnected, and that our actions can have an impact on each other.

We need to develop a respect for differences, and learn to accommodate for different priorities that may be based on those differences. In addition, we need to learn to collaborate both person to person, and government to government, to arrive at solutions that will enrich the common good.

How Do We Develop the Skills Needed to Meet the Challenges of a Global World?

The first step is to develop an awareness of the social issues that impact a global society. These issues include equity, human rights, treatment of minorities, and cultural diversity. Individuals are sometimes hindered in their understanding of others by their fear and apprehension of those who are different from them. We often fear what we do not know. Therefore, we must begin to learn about other cultures and environments that are different from our own.

Understanding diversity involves **awareness**, **tolerance**, and **acceptance**. It requires that you do the following:
- Become aware of your own biases.
- Monitor your behaviors/attitudes.

- Be willing to change/adapt/modify your perceptions, beliefs, and attitudes.
- Accept that there are other ways of knowing and being.
- Embrace the differences of others without judgment or prejudice.

The "Global" Workplace

Globalization is changing the face of the workplace. Increasingly women, minorities, and individuals from other cultures and religions are entering the workforce at every level of employment in this country. Women are taking on leadership roles as CEOs of Fortune 500 companies, to running for the presidency of the United States. Individuals from other cultures, who are in professional or management positions, may have perspectives on work ethics and time management that differ from the "American" perspective. These differing viewpoints will have to be understood, and worked through so that employers and employees can function effectively as a team.

The necessity of understanding diversity is so great that the majority of businesses, industries, and educational institutions offer diversity training for their employees on a continuous basis.

Multicultural Terms

The following terms clarify and help define the nuances of diversity.

Pluralism refers to a coexistence of distinct ethnic and cultural groups in the same society.
Social distance is when people should maintain a certain distance from each other. The appropriate distances may vary from culture to culture.
Culture refers to the behavior, patterns, beliefs, and all other products of a particular group of people that are passed on from generation to generation.
Prejudice is an unjustified negative attitude toward an individual based on the individual's membership in a group.
Culture shock refers to the disorganizing effects of being exposed to unfamiliar ways of life.
Integration refers to maintaining cultural integrity while becoming an integral part of the larger culture.
Acculturation refers to cultural changes that result from continuous firsthand contact between two distinctive cultural groups, but that preserves the identities of both.

Ethnic identity is a sense of membership based on ethnicity.

Marginalization is a process in which groups are put out of contact with both their traditional culture and the larger dominant culture.

Stereotype is a generalization about a group's characteristics that does not consider any variation from one member of the group to the next.

Multiculturalism promotes a pluralistic approach to understanding two or more different cultures, and implies that people can maintain their identities while working with others to form different cultures.

Discrimination occurs when prejudice leads to differential treatment based on an individual's membership in a group.

Racism is a belief that members of another race or ethnic group are inferior.

Assimilation occurs when individuals relinquish their cultural identity and move into the larger society.

Diaspora is any group that has been dispersed outside its traditional homeland, or any religious group living as a minority among people of the prevailing religion.

Misogyny is hatred, distrust, or mistrust of women.

Ethnic ambiguity encompasses multiracial individuals age 30 and under, with racially indeterminate looks.

Xenophobia is an unreasonable fear or hatred of foreigners or strangers, or of that which is foreign or strange.

Diversity and You

How do you begin to increase or enhance your understanding of diversity? One way is to gather as much information as possible about different populations. This research can be done by delving into the vast amount of information available in books, articles, music, the Internet, and the most moving and powerful of the mediums, feature films. At the end of this section, there is a short list of films that cover some of the different aspects of diversity.

Another way to learn about a specific population is to write an autobiography from the perspective of someone from a different culture, race, religion, age, gender, nationality, sexual preference, social class, or with a disability. By performing this exercise, you would need to dig deep into the essence of the individual. This exercise works at creating empathy and understanding within the writer.

One of the best methods to understand diversity is to totally immerse yourself into the culture of the population that you want to understand. If given the opportunity, travel abroad and spend time in another country, or spend time in this country with someone from another culture or race. Walk the walk and talk the talk. As the old adage goes, "You must walk a mile in someone's shoes before you can judge them."

Globalization has turned the world into a global village. Embracing diversity in the workplace and in your daily life is a necessity in the twenty-first century. It is a necessity that can bring enrichment and enlightenment to your life and experiences.

We end this chapter with a poem by American poet James Patrick Kinney, titled 'The Cold Within." The poem was written in the 1960s during the height of the civil rights movement. At the time, this poem was considered too controversial to be published in the *Saturday Evening Post* magazine.

The Cold Within

Six humans trapped by happenstance
In bleak and bitter cold.
Each one possessed a stick of wood
Or so the story's told.

Their dying fire in need of logs
The first man held his back
For of the faces round the fire
He noticed one was black.

The next man looking 'cross the way
Saw one not of his church
And couldn't bring himself to give
The fire his stick of birch.

The third one sat in tattered clothes,
He gave his coat a hitch.
Why should his log be put to use
To warm the idle rich?

The rich man just sat back and thought
Of the wealth he had in store
And how to keep what he had earned
From the lazy shiftless poor.

The black man's face bespoke revenge
As the fire passed from his sight.
For all he saw in his stick of wood
Was a chance to spite the white.

The last man of this forlorn group
Did nought except to gain.
Giving only to those who gave
Was how he played the game.

Their logs held tight in death's still hands
Was proof of human sin.
They didn't die from the cold without
They died from the cold within.

—James Patrick Kinney

REFERENCES AND RECOMMENDED READINGS:

Albrecht, K. (2005). *Social Intelligence: The New Science of Success; Beyond IQ, Beyond EI, Applying Multiple Intelligence Theory to Human Interaction.* New York: Jossey-Bass.
The Cold Within, http://en.wikipedia.org/wiki/The_Cold_Within (public domain).
Goleman, D. (2006). *Social Intelligence: The Revolutionary New Science of Human Relationships.* New York: Bantam Books.
Goleman, D. (2013). *Focus: The Hidden Driver of Excellence.* HarperCollins. New York
Sternberg, R.J. (2000). *Handbook of Intelligence* (2nd ed., pp. 359–379). Cambridge, UK: Cambridge University Press.

RECOMMENDED FILMS:

Race:
The Hurricane (Rubin Carter story)
Mississippi Burning
Schindler's List
Miss Evers' Boys
Glory
12 Years a Slave

A Time to Kill
Gung Ho!
To Kill a Mockingbird
Roots
Something the Lord Made

Race/Gender:
Beloved
The Color Purple
The Joy Luck Club
The Danish Girl
Normal

Sexual Preference:
And the Band Played On
Philadelphia
Torch Song Trilogy
Birdcage

Age:
Cocoon
These Old Broads
Grumpy Old Men
Best Exotic Marigold Hotel and The Second Best Exotic Marigold Hotel

Reflective FOCUS

▼ How does civility fit into the picture of a person who has social intelligence?

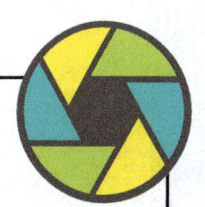

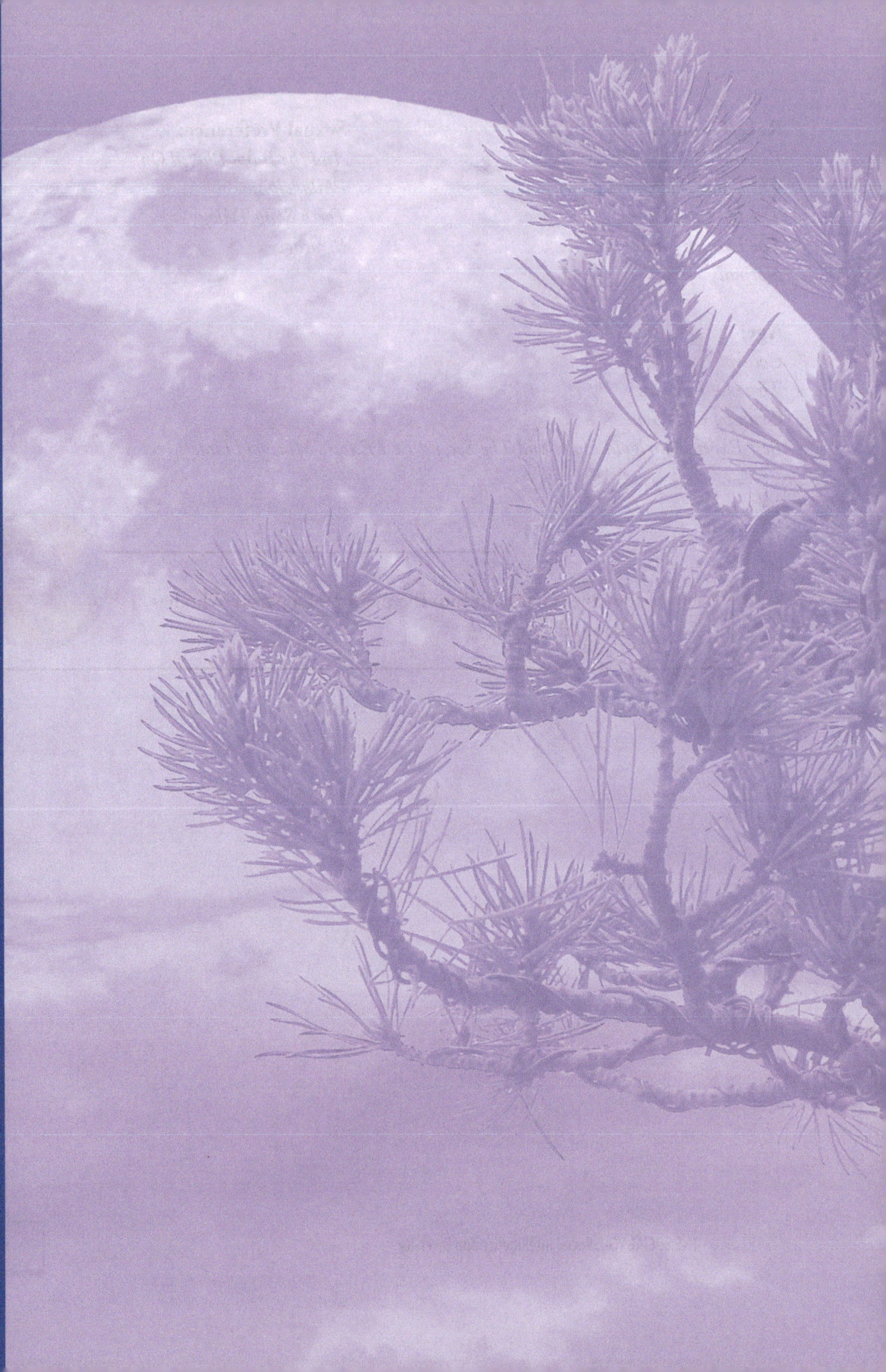

PART III
Looking Within

Image © Eugene Sergeev, 2014. Used under license from Shutterstock, Inc.

Odysseus travels to the underworld to see the blind seer, Teiresias. Teiresias tells him that the way home has been there the whole time; he just needs to see it. When he finally realizes he is a prisoner of his own desires, Odysseus is able to return home to Ithaca.

In this part, you will use assessments to "look within" and uncover your personality preferences and interests. You can discover what is important to you through identifying your personal and work values. The work of Carl Jung's psychological types sheds light on the relationship of personality type and career choice, as well as interpersonal relationships. In order to find the "right fit" career, you must look at all three components—personality, interests, and values—and how they interrelate to determine the path that supports your passion.

chapter 8
Personality Type and You

"Your vision will become clear only when you look into your own heart."

–Carl Jung

Swiss psychiatrist Carl Jung was once considered the heir apparent to the father of psychoanalysis, Sigmund Freud. However, Jung's path was derailed when he became critical of Freud's concepts and departed to focus on his own theory of analytic psychology. Jung's departure led to the development of his theories of psychological type.

The theory of psychological type had its genesis in Jung's observations of his patients who came in for psychotherapy. He noticed similar patterns of behavior, characteristics, thinking styles, and reactions among his patients whether they were male or female, young or old, Christians or Jews, Swiss or Italian. After analyzing these patterns, Jung felt that he could predict the behaviors of individuals who shared these common traits. Equipped with this knowledge as a tool, he thought he could better understand, guide, and help his patients.

Jung's Psychological Types

Jung's theory of type had eight elements that were used in combination to identify an individual's personality type. The first element had to do with what he called the **thinking function**—that is, the way a person perceives and processes information. The four thinking functions are thinking, feeling, sensing, and intuition. **Thinking** was defined as logical and analytical. **Feeling** was described as sensing the emotional value of an event or relationship. **Sensing** was thought of as concrete doing. Sensing people tend to be practical and prefer hands-on activities. **Intuition** was seen as an abstract way of processing, identifying, and solving problems that lacked concrete and logical substance (e.g., an inner knowing or "gut" feeling that occurred without facts to support the knowledge).

The second element dealt with the direction in which people focused their energy. Jung coined these terms for the two directions: **introversion** and **extraversion**. He saw introverts as focusing inwardly, and deriving energy from going within. He viewed extraverts as those focusing outwardly, and deriving energy from the external environment.

FIGURE 8.1: Introvert and Extravert

The third aspect of his theory related to the idea that a person has an innately preferred lead cerebral function. Another way of saying this is, individuals have a genetic predisposition to use one of the four thinking functions: thinking, feeling, sensing, intuition. A natural thinker would look to find a logical, structural relationship between things in order to make choices. A natural feeler would look for harmony, and to feel connected to elements in his or her environment. A natural sensor would seek order and established procedures. A natural intuitive would look for the "big picture" patterns.

FIGURE 8.2: Intuitive

Combining Types

Jung then combined a person's preferred brain lead (cerebral function) with his or her preferred direction (introversion or extraversion). Thus, a person could be an introverted feeler or an extraverted feeler; an introverted thinker or an extraverted thinker; an introverted sensor or an extraverted sensor; and an introverted intuitive or an extraverted intuitive.

According to psychological type theory, individuals would develop the skills, capabilities, and gifts associated with their natural (preferred) lead functions, in an environment consistent with their preferred direction (introversion or extraversion). Jung defined falsification of type as any situation in which a person developed, and used (for a long period), skills and abilities associated with a function other than their preferred function. Jung believed that people who lived their lives by operating from a nonpreferred function ran the risk of diminished self-esteem, identity confusion, health problems, and a lack of synchronicity in supporting their life and chosen career path. Here is an example: If a person's natural

CHAPTER 8: Personality Type and You

lead function is feeling (prefers harmony and affiliation) and the person for whatever reason conducts his or her life as a thinker (logical, objective, impersonal) for an extended period of time, the health and well-being of the individual will be compromised.

The ultimate goal of understanding psychological type is for the individual to (a) enhance and develop his or her preferred function and energy direction to a very high degree; (b) develop the nonpreferred function and energy direction to a lesser degree; and (c) arrive at a place of transcendence. In Jung's estimation, transcendence was the state of being fully self-actualized.

FIGURE 8.3: Sensor

"I am not what happened to me, I am what I choose to become."

—Carl Jung

Myers-Briggs Type Indicator—MBTI

In the mid-1930s, Isabel Myers-Briggs and Katherine Briggs set out to design a psychological instrument based on Jung's theory of psychological type. The end result of their design efforts was the Myers-Briggs Type Indicator, or MBTI.

The MBTI identifies eight preferences: introversion, extraversion, sensing, intuition, thinking, feeling, judging, and perceiving. Sensing, intuition, thinking, and feeling are cognitive functions (Jung's cerebral leads). Extraversion, introversion, judging, and perceiving are called attitudes. Extraversion and introversion, as Jung originally calculated, have to do with direction of energy. Judging and perceiving, which were not part of Jung's psychological type theory, represent a person's orientation to the world.

The preferences are paired, and an individual will have a genetic predisposition for one aspect of each pair. A person will either be:

Extraverted (E) or Introverted (I)
Sensing (S) or Intuitive (N)
Feeling (F) or Thinking (T)
Judging (J) or Perceiving (P)

ISFP

Sixteen Types

There are sixteen possible personality types, with four letters representing each type. A person who demonstrates a preference for extraversion, intuition, thinking, and perceiving would be an ENTP. Each of the sixteen personality types has its own unique constellation of characteristics and behaviors.

Extraversion and **introversion** represent how people **interact with the world,** and the way they prefer to **receive stimulation and energy**. **Extraverts** are stimulated by interacting with the outside world of people and things. **Introverts** are energized by the internal world of their own ideas and thoughts.

Sensing and **intuition** represent the way people **prefer to gather data**. **Sensors** are very practical, hands-on type of people who prefer specific answers to specific questions. They rely on their five senses to obtain information about the world. **Intuitives** obtain information about the world by looking at the "big picture," seeing possibilities, making connections between disparate parts, and trusting their gut feelings.

The way individuals **prefer to make decisions** is reflected in a preference for **thinking** or **feeling**. **Thinkers** use logic, data, and objectivity to make decisions. **Feelers** use a subjective value system to make decisions, are very aware of other people's feelings, and seek harmony in most situations.

The manner in which people **prefer to orient their lives** (structured or

FIGURE 8.4: Thinker

Image © Rido, 2014. Used under license from Shutterstock, Inc.

CHAPTER 8: Personality Type and You

89

spontaneous and adaptive), is found in preference for **judging** or **perceiving**. **Judgers** seek order, control, and predictability in their lives. **Perceivers** prefer no rules, fluidity, adventure, and, above all, options.

See the "Personality Type and Careers" chart at the end of this chapter for career ideas.

MBTI and Career Choice

One of the essential elements in career choice is finding a career that is the "right fit" with a person's basic nature. There is an enormous expenditure of energy in trying to fit a person into a career that does not match his or her core values.

In the MBTI, an individual's core values can be identified through the concept of **temperament type**. The classification of different temperament types has existed since medieval times. At that time people were categorized as **choleric** (driven, powerful, and dominant), **sanguine** (expressive, adaptable, and friendly), **phlegmatic** (methodical, intellectual, and dutiful), or **melancholic** (analytical, dedicated, and intense). Today with the MBTI, individuals are identified via their two dominant functions/attitudes:

SJ–Sensing/Judging
SP–Sensing/Perceiving
NF–Intuitive/Feeling
NT—Intuitive/Thinking

Each of these temperament types will flourish in different work settings. Understanding one's temperament type allows the individual to match his or her core values with the values and functions of a particular career.

FIGURE 8.5: Feeler

MBTI TEMPERAMENT TYPES

TYPE	VALUE	BEST FIT
SJ Sensing/Judging	• Being down to earth and decisive • Structured and orderly • Tradition, rules, and regulations • Security • Serving society	• Stable company that provides high level of responsibility • Managerial positions • Environment with regulations and rewards • Gravitate to criminal justice field
SP Sensing/Perceiving	• Being responsive and spontaneous • "Hands on" • Focusing on here and now • Less structure • Acting on their impulses • Being action oriented	• Career that provides variety, autonomy, action and immediate results • Opportunity to troubleshoot • Careers that allow use of acquired skills, often involving tools
NF Intuitive/Feeling	• Possibilities, meanings, relationships • Personal growth, self understanding • Motivating others • Searching for meaning of life • Initiating change • Communications	• Career that is personally meaningful • Want to be part of organization that values people • Tend to gravitate towards human resources jobs, teaching, counseling, consulting, the arts
NT Intuitive/Thinking	• Solving complex problems through seeing possibilities • Making decisions impersonally and logically • Independence and curiosity • Setting high standards for self • Designing change	• Careers that provide autonomy and variety • Chance to propose ideas and use their intellect • Careers that allow showing competency • Leadership positions such as; College professor, management, fields of science, computers, medicine, law

CHAPTER 8: Personality Type and You

FIGURE 8.6: Perceiver

FIGURE 8.7: Judger

Personality Type and You

Knowing and understanding your personality type gives you a greater awareness of yourself and others, and facilitates positive relationships, both personally and professionally. It provides you with a basis for understanding the similarities between people and developing an appreciation for the differences. A personality assessment provides valuable information that can be employed in selecting a career that will resonate with your personality preferences.

Understanding your personality closely aligns with one of Maslow's attributes of self-actualization—that is, greatly increased creativeness. This contends that individuals will have an inborn uniqueness that carries over into everything they do. They will also be more inventive and less inhibited.

Once understanding their personalities, individuals will have a better understanding and appreciation of self and be able to then look at others and appreciate them for their own beauty and uniqueness. In embracing one's uniqueness, individuals increase their capacity for creativity and inventiveness.

Jung believed that people, in the course of their lifetime, would develop both their preferred and nonpreferred personality characteristics, and that the end result would be their achieving transcendence or self-actualization.

REFERENCES AND RECOMMENDED READINGS:

Jung, C.G. (1968). *The Archetypes and the Collective Unconscious.* New York: Princeton University Press.

Kroeger, O., & Thuesen, J. (1988). *Type Talk*. New York: Tilden Press.

Kroeger, O., & Thuesen, J. (1992). *Type Talk at Work*. New York: Tilden Press.

Tieger, P., & Barron-Tieger, B. (1992). *Do What You Are: Discover the Perfect Career for You Through the Secrets of Personality Type*. New York: Little, Brown, and Company.

MBTI's Personality Types with Correlating Careers

ESTP	ESTJ	ENTP	ENTJ
real estate broker	government employee	systems designer	program designer
chef	pharmaceutical sales	venture capitalist	attorney
land developer	auditor	actor	administrator
physical therapist	computer analyst	journalist	office manager
stock broker	technical trainer	investment broker	chemical engineer
news reporter	project manager	real estate agent	sales manager
firefighter	officer manager	real estate developer	logistics consultant
promoter	factory supervisor	strategic planner	franchise owner
entrepreneur	credit analyst	political manager	new business developer
pilot	electrical engineer	politician	personnel manager
budget analyst	stockbroker	special projects developer	investment banker
insurance agent	regulatory compliance	literary agent	labor relations
management consultant	officer	restaurant/bar owner	management trainer
franchise owner	chief information officer	technical trainer	credit investigator
electrical engineer	construction worker	diversity manager	mortgage broker
aircraft mechanic	general contractor	art director	corporate team trainer
technical trainer	paralegal	personnel systems	environmental engineer
EEG technologist	industrial engineer	developer	biomedical engineer
radiological technician	budget analyst	computer analyst	business consultant
emergency medical tech.	data base manager	logistics consultant	educational consultant
corrections officer	funeral director	outplacement consultant	personal financial planner
flight attendant	cook	advertising creative	network integration
	security guard	director	specialist
		radio/TV talk show	

CHAPTER 8: Personality Type and You

ESFP	ESFJ	ENFP	ENFJ
veterinarian	nurse	conference planner	entertainer
flight attendant	social worker	speech pathologist	recruiter
floral designer	caterer	HR development trainer	artist
real estate agent	flight attendant	ombudsman	newscaster
child care provider	bookkeeper	clergy	writer/journalist
social worker	medical/dental assistant	journalist	recreation director
fundraiser	exercise physiologist	newscaster	librarian
athletic coach	elementary school teacher	career counselor	facilitator
musician	minister/priest/rabbi	housing director	politician
secretary	retail owner	character actor	psychologist
receptionist	officer manager	marketing consultant	housing director
special events producer	telemarketer	musician/composer	career counselor
teacher: preschool	counselor	artist	sales trainer
teacher: elementary	special education teacher	graphics designer	travel agent
emergency room nurse	merchandise planner	human resource manager	program designer
occupational therapist	credit counselor	merchandise planner	corporate/team trainer
exercise physiologist	athletic coach	advertising account manager	child welfare worker
team trainer	insurance agent	dietitian/nutritionist	social worker interpreter/ translator
travel sales	sales representative	massage therapist	occupational therapist
public relations specialist	massage therapist	editor/art director	executive: small business
waiter/waitress	medical secretary	writer/poet/novelist	alcohol/drug counselor
labor relations mediator	child care provider		sales manager
	bilingual education teacher		
	professional volunteer		

ISTP	ISTJ	INTP	INTJ
surveyor	accounting	strategic planning	management consultant
firefighter	auditing	writer	economist
private investigator	efficiency expert	staff development	scientist
pilot	engineer	lawyer	computer programmer
police officer	geologist	architect	environmental planner
purchasing agent	bank examiners	software designer	new business developer
chiropractor	organization	financial analyst	curriculum designer
medical technician	development	college professor	administrator
securities analyst	electricians	photographer	mathematician
computer repair person	dentists	logician	psychologist
race car driver	pharmacist	artist	neurologist
computer programmer	school principals	systems analyst	biomedical researcher
electrical engineer	school bus drivers	neurologist	strategic planner
legal secretary	file clerk	physicist	civil engineer
coach/trainer	stock broker	psychologist	intellectual properties
commercial artist	legal secretary	research/development	attorney
carpenter	computer operator	specialist	designer
paralegal	computer programmer	computer programmer	editor/art director
dental assistant	technical writer	data base manager	inventor
radiological technician	chief information officer	chemist	informational-graphics
marine biologist	police officer	biologist	designer
software developer	real estate agent	investigator	financial planner
management			judge

CHAPTER 8: Personality Type and You

Introverted, Sensing, Feeling, Perceiving

ISFP	ISFJ	INFP	INFJ
bookkeeper	counseling	graphics designer	career counselor
clerical supervisor	ministry	college professor	writer/poet/novelist
dental assistant	library work	researcher	clinical psychologist
physical therapist	nursing	legal mediator	environmental lawyer
mechanic	secretarial	social worker	teacher: HS or college: --
radiology technologist	curators	holistic health	arts, drama
surveyor	bookkeepers	practitioner	special or early education
chef	dental hygienists	occupational therapist	social worker
forester	computer operator	diversity manager	interior designer
geologist	personnel administrator	human resource	graphics designer
landscaper designer	paralegal	development specialist	artist
crisis hotline operator	real estate agent	employment	director of religious
teacher: elementary	artist	development	education
beautician	interior decorator	specialist	project manager
typist	retail owner	minister/priest/rabbi	health care administrator
jeweler	musician	missionary	chiropractor
gardener	elementary school	psychologist	dietitian/nutritionist
potter	teacher	writer/poet/novelist	legal mediator
painter	physical therapist	journalist	human resources
botanist	nurse	editor/art director	manager
marine biologist	social worker	organizational	coach
	personnel counselor	development	desktop publisher/editor
	alcohol/drug counselor	specialist	art director

Go to this website for a free Myers-Briggs Type Indicator assessment: www.humanmetrics.com

SUIT Yourself
The Secret of Career Satisfaction

It's important to find the right job. Despite the universal fantasy of winning the lottery, buying expensive cars and homes, and doing fascinating work with interesting people in exotic places, the sober reality is that most of us have to work, hard, for a long time. If you spend forty to fifty years - not an unlikely scenario -working at jobs you'd rather not be doing, you are in truth throwing away a large part of your life. This is unnecessary and sad, especially since a career you can love is within your reach.

What Is the Ideal Job, Anyway? The right job enhances your life. It is personally fulfilling because it nourishes the most important aspects of your personality. It suits the way you like to do things and reflects who you are. It lets you use your innate strengths in ways that come naturally to you, and it doesn't force you to do things you don't do well (at least, not often!).

How can you tell if you're in the right job? Here are some general guidelines. If you're not employed, keep them in mind as you search for your ideal job. If you are employed, see how your present job measures up.

If you're in the right job, you should:

- Look forward to going to work
- Feel energized (most of the time) by what you do
- Feel your contribution is respected and appreciated
- Feel proud when describing your work to others
- Enjoy and respect the people you work with
- Feel optimistic about your future

We'd like to make something clear right away. It's important to recognize that there are as many different paths to career satisfaction as there are happily employed people. There is no one "ideal job" to which everyone should aspire. But there is an ideal job *for you*.

There are an infinite number of variables in the workplace. To achieve career satisfaction you need to figure out what your preferences are and then find a job that accommodates them. Some jobs provide warmth and stability; some are risky and challenging. Some are structured, some aren't. One job may require a lot of socializing, while another may require quiet concentration. Do you know exactly what kind of job suits you best? Have you ever even stopped to think about it?

It's a good thing there are so many different kinds of jobs available, since people are so different in their abilities and priorities. Some people enjoy making high-level management decisions; others simply aren't suited to making these kinds of choices. For some people, money is a top priority. They want to make lots of it! Others, however, want most to make a contribution to society; the money is less important. Some people are perfectly comfortable with facts and details and statistics, while others get a headache just trying to read a profit-and-loss statement. And so on, and so on!

When we were hired to conduct a series of personal effectiveness training workshops for job placement professionals (also known as executive recruiters or headhunters), we came face-to-face with a dramatic example of how a job that is perfect for one person can be perfectly wrong for another.

We were training several headhunters who worked for the same recruiting firm. Their job was to find applicants to fill positions at a variety of companies by calling people who were already employed and convincing them to apply for these positions. If an applicant successfully switched jobs and stayed with the new company for at least three months, the placement counselor received a generous commission. It was a highly competitive, results-oriented job that required excellent communication skills and the ability to fill as many positions as possible as quickly as possible.

One of the placement counselors we trained, Arthur, couldn't have been happier. He loved the fast pace of the job. Arthur was a high-energy person, a great talker who enjoyed meeting lots of people over the phone. He used his excellent reasoning skills to persuade other people to make a move to a new opportunity, and he got a lot of satisfaction out of meeting his goal and then some. Arthur knew and understood the formula: for every fifty calls he made, he'd get ten people who were interested, and out of these ten, he might make two or three placements. Arthur's "thick skin" helped him in the job because he often heard "no" during the day, but he never took the rejection personally. What Arthur found really energizing was closing the sale and moving on to the next challenge. He worked hard all day long and made a lot of money.

For Julie, it was a totally different story. Unlike Arthur, Julie enjoyed talking to lots of people all day and establishing relationships with them. However, unlike Arthur, Julie wanted to help each person find the job that would be really right for him or her. She liked to look for opportunities that would enable her applicants to grow and experience personal success and satisfaction. Julie had been cautioned repeatedly by her supervisor about spending too much time on the phone with each individual rather than quickly determining whether or not someone was interested in a position and then moving on to the next prospect. Rather than filing jobs, Julie was counseling clients. The fact that she could make a great deal of money did not motivate her. She found little reward in simply filling a job opening with a person who probably wasn't right for the position but whom she had successfully pressured into giving it a try.

When we returned six weeks later for a follow-up training session, we weren't surprised to learn that Julie had quit.

People are different in their needs, desires, interests, skills, values and personalities. Unless you and I have similar personality types, work that you find intrinsically enjoyable is likely to have a different, even opposite, effect on me. Different jobs and even different aspects of jobs satisfy different types of people, a fundamental truth which has, in our view, not been fully appreciated by career advisers or career manuals — until now.

To Suit Yourself, You Must Know Yourself

As we said earlier, the secret of career satisfaction lies in doing what you enjoy most. A few lucky people discover this secret early in life, but most of us are caught in a kind of psychological wrestling match, torn between what we think we *can* do, what we (or others) feel we *ought* to do, and what we think we *want* to do. Our advice? Concentrate instead on *who you are*, and the rest will fall into place.

Not long ago, a friend called us. She calls all the time — there's a phone in practically every room of her home — but this was more than a social call. Ellen was mad. A co-worker of hers whom she regarded as "more boring than a turnip" had been given a prime assignment designing a complex computer system for a growing retail chain.

Ellen, who had been hired just six months before to do exactly this kind of work, was stunned. Obviously something was wrong — but what?

Ellen had evaluated her new job with the utmost care before accepting it. She had both the analytical ability and the background experience the job required. She was well liked and found the technical aspects of the job challenging. She'd had a series of unsatisfying jobs before, but this one was going to be different. So why was her golden opportunity turning to brass? Worse. . . why was the turnip doing better than she?

We thought we knew the answer. Ellen's co-worker, as she described him, was absolutely content to work long hours in relative isolation, quietly but steadily getting the job done. He wasn't a lot of fun around the office, but he was intelligent and dependable, and he never made waves. He was, in fact, the perfect person for the job - and he was happy doing it.

Ellen, on the other hand, loved the stimulation of rallying her staff for an urgent deadline and enjoyed talking to clients about their needs. She was terrific at explaining the intricacies of computer systems and could charm people into doing remarkable things. She liked going to industry conferences, and she didn't mind spending all day in meetings. Unfortunately, none of these activities were a significant part of her new position.

It was clear to us that even though Ellen could handle her responsibilities adequately, the job required more solitude, concentration, and what we call "task focus" than she liked. As she talked things through (and some people are like that — they like to think out loud), she began to recognize that in all her careful planning she had overlooked just one thing. . . her own personality!

At this point in our conversation, Ellen panicked. She was afraid she had spent eight years in the wrong career. No wonder she'd found her previous jobs less than thrilling! However, she wasn't actually in the wrong field — she was just working in the wrong end of it. Today Ellen has moved over into the sales division of the same company and is thriving in her new position.

Perhaps a little experiment will clarify what we're talking about. On a piece of paper, or even in the margin, write your signature. Done? OK. Now do the same thing, using your opposite hand. (If you just groaned, you are not alone; most people have a similar reaction.) How did it feel when you used your preferred hand? Most people use words like "natural," "easy," "quick," "effortless." How did it feel when you used the opposite hand? Some typical responses: "slow," "awkward," "hard," "draining," "tiring," "it took much longer," "it required more energy and concentration."

We think that handedness is a good way to think about using your natural strengths in your work. The use of your preferred hand is comfortable and assured. If you were forced to use your other hand, you could no doubt develop your abilities - but using that hand would never be as effortless as using your preferred hand, and the finished product would never be as skillfully executed.

The Traditional Approach and Why it Doesn't Work

Career professionals have long been aware that certain kinds of people are better at certain types of jobs, and that it's important to find as good a match as possible between the person you are and the kind of job you choose. The problem is that the traditional approach doesn't take enough considerations into account. The conventional analysis looks at only the "big three": your abilities, interests, and values.

As career counselors ourselves, we recognize the importance of these factors. Certainly you need the right skills to perform a job well. It also helps if you're interested in your work. And it's important to feel good about what you do. But this is far from the whole picture! Your personality has additional dimensions that also need to be recognized. As a general rule, the more aspects of your personality you match to your work, the more satisfied you'll be on the job.

As we saw with Ellen, a vital consideration—often overlooked—is how much stimulation from other people you need in your work. Are you more energized by being around lots of people most of the time, or are you more comfortable in small groups, talking one-on-one, or maybe working alone? You can see what a profound impact this preference can have upon your choice of a job. Other important factors include the kind of information you naturally notice, the way you make decisions, and whether you prefer to live in a more structured or a more spontaneous way. These preferences reflect mental processes that are basic to every human being but that clearly differ from one personality type to another. Trying to find the best job for you without taking these preferences into account is like trying to find a tiny island in the vast ocean without a chart. With luck, you might get there—but you might not!

Joanne was a client of ours who came to us in a career crisis. At the age of thirty, she was at the end of her rope. After seven years of teaching math at the elementary school level she was completely burned out and was wondering if she was in the right career.

Being a teacher had seemed the most natural thing in the world for Joanne. The eldest of four, she had grown up taking care of children. She had excelled in math throughout school and was interested in education. Joanne had received some career counseling early on, and all the signs had seemed to point in the same direction. In high school, and again in college, Joanne had taken the standard career aptitude tests and assessment instruments to determine her skills, her interests, and her values. Each time, career counselors had encouraged her to obtain a teaching degree and to teach math to young kids. Everything seemed perfect.

After her first challenging year Joanne became increasingly frustrated with the rigid structure of the public elementary school setting. She disliked the endless rules both she and the students had to live by as well as many of the rules she had to enforce. She hated having to prepare lesson plans six weeks in advance that left her unable to respond to the interests of the children and to her own creative inspirations. She found the standard workbooks inane, and the busywork that both she and her students were required to do left her drained and irritated. Joanne felt very isolated because her colleagues all seemed to have interests and values that were not like hers, and she began to discover that she missed the intellectual stimulation of working on challenging projects with her intellectual equals. She had tried switching grades and even changing schools, but nothing seemed to help.

After talking with us, Joanne was relieved to discover that she wasn't crazy; she was just in the wrong career. As her early counselors had determined, Joanne had many of the right qualifications for teaching. However, the things she found most stimulating—intellectual challenge, opportunities to raise her level of competence, and creative innovation—were totally lacking in her job. Moreover, the public school setting forced her to work in a highly-structured and detailed way, which was not at all the way she liked to operate.

Luckily, the solution quickly became clear. We suggested that Joanne return to school and obtain a master's degree in order to teach math—still a thriving interest of hers—in higher education. In a college setting, she would be able to enjoy much more flexibility in her work schedule and obligations, teach more complicated courses, and be part of an intellectual environment.

Joanne did get a master's degree, and shortly thereafter she accepted a position in the math department of a small college. Today she teaches graduate-level math courses while continuing her studies toward obtaining a Ph.D.

There's also another reason why the traditional approach to career counseling is inadequate. The "big three" — your abilities, interests, and values—all change with age. As you gain work experience, you gain new skills. As you live longer, you may pick up new interests and discard old ones. And often your goals are different later in life than they were earlier. You can keep changing your career according to where you find yourself at a particular point in time, or you can base your choice from the beginning on a deeper understanding of who you are (and who you'll always be!)

Alex is a thirty-nine-year-old internist with a successful practice in a Chicago suburb. While he was growing up it was always assumed that he would follow in the family tradition and become a doctor. Through twelve years of college, medical school, internship, and residency, he never allowed himself to question his decision. After practicing medicine for five years, he has come to a painful conclusion with far-reaching implications for himself and his family: he doesn't want to be a doctor any more. What's more, he realizes he probably never did.

Alex's predicament is not unusual. If you doubt this, pick any ten people you know and ask them, "If you could have any job you wanted, what would it be?" Our experience as career counselors suggests that at least *half* would rather be doing something else.

Most of us make our most important career decisions when we are least prepared to do so. The decisions we make early in life set into motion a chain of events that will influence our entire lives. Yet when we're young we have little or no experience making job choices, and we tend to have an overabundance of idealistic enthusiasm, plus a reckless lack of concern for future consequences. We haven't lived long enough to see ourselves tested in a variety of situations, and we're highly susceptible to bad advice from well-intentioned parents, teachers, counselors, or friends. No wonder so many people get off to a poor start.

The solution? To achieve as great a degree of self-awareness as you can before making any decision with long-lasting career consequences. Happily, "finding yourself" does not require a guru, a lot of money, or any period of experimentation.

You Can't Help It –You Were Born that Way!

Since the right job flows directly out of all the elements of your personality type, you need to spend some time figuring out what makes you tick. By making a conscious effort to discover the "real you," you can learn how to focus your natural strengths and inclinations into a career you can love for as long as you choose to work, This is where Type is so helpful. It provides a systematic, effective way to evaluate both your strong points and your probable weaknesses or blind spots. Once you have these figured out, you'll know how to make sure you are always operating from a position of strength. Each of us has a distinct personality, like an innate blueprint that stays with us for life. We are born with a personality type, we go through life with that type, and when we are laid to rest (hopefully at the end of a long and fruitful life), it is with the same type.

Now you are probably wondering, "Wait a minute. I might be one way sometimes, but at other times I'm a very different person. Doesn't the situation influence my personality type?"

The answer is no, it doesn't. Do we change our behavior in certain situations? Certainly! Most human beings have a tremendous repertoire of behaviors available to them. We couldn't function very successfully if we didn't. Sure, we act differently at work than we do at home, and it makes a difference whether we're with strangers, close friends, at a ball park, or at a funeral. But people don't change their basic personalities with every new door they walk through.

All this is not to say that environmental factors are not extremely important; they are. Parents, siblings, teachers, and economic, social, and political circumstances all can play a role in determining what directions our lives take.

Some people are forced by circumstances to act in a certain way until they are literally "not themselves" (more about this later). But we all start off with a particular personality type that predisposes us to behave in certain ways for our entire lives.

If you are skeptical about the idea that personality type is inborn, take a look at different children from the same family. These could be your own children, your siblings, or even children from a family you know. Do they have different personalities? You bet they do, and often the differences are apparent from birth (or even in utero).

The concept of "personality type" is not new. People have always been aware of the similarities and differences between individuals, and over the centuries many systems and models for understanding or categorizing these differences have been developed. Today, our understanding of human behavior has been expanded to such a degree that we are now able to accurately identify sixteen distinctly different personality types.

Finding the right job for each of these distinct personalities may seem like an awesome task. However, all sixteen personality types do function in the world. As we will see, it is possible to identify your own personality type and the types of others, to understand why certain types flourish in certain kinds of jobs, and to clarify why people find career satisfaction in different ways.

From "Do What You Are, Fifth Edition" by Paul D. Tieger and Barbara Barron-Tieger. Copyright © 1992, 1995, 2001, 2007, 2014 by Paul D. Tieger and Barbara Barron-Tieger. Used by of Little, Brown and Company. All rights reserved.

Reflective FOCUS

▼ Why is it important to "know ourselves"?

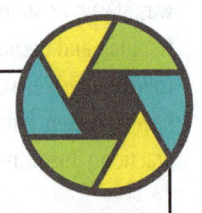

chapter 9
Connecting the Dots

INTERESTS AND VALUES

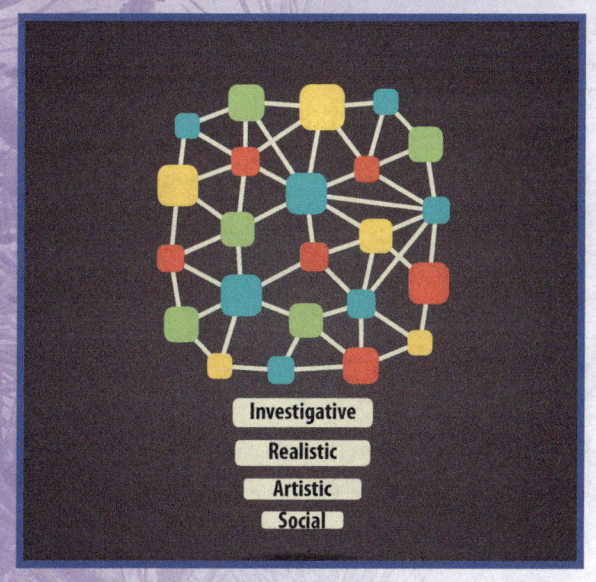

"Success is liking yourself, liking what you do, and liking how you do it."

–Maya Angelou, poet

Adapted image © vectoraart, 2014. Used under license from Shutterstock, Inc.

John loves to go the movies. Mary jumps at the chance to hike in the woods and identify species of plants. Joe spends every free minute tinkering with his car.

All three of these individuals have a passion for their chosen activity. The activities and subjects that attract a person's interest can be powerful predictors of career suitability.

People tend to seek situations in which they can use their skills and talents to express themselves positively. Often, individuals who share similar personality traits are drawn to the same vocations. Choosing a career involves an alignment of one's values, personality preferences, abilities, and interests. If a career choice meets only the value requirements of an individual, and he or she has no interest or ability in the chosen field; ultimately the person will be unhappy with the job and will look for a more appropriate work setting.

Identifying one's interests, and discovering the relationship between those interests and the world of work, is crucial in successful career planning.

Holland Codes

Interest inventory assessments generally identify six personality types. These types are called the **Holland Codes**. The codes are as follows: **realistic, investigative, artistic, social, enterprising,** and **conventional (RIASEC)**.

FIGURE 9.1: Realistic

FIGURE 9.2: Investigative

FIGURE 9.3: Artistic

FIGURE 9.4: Social

Realistic (R) types like to work with objects, tools, machines, and animals. Careers include farmer, police officer, carpenter, and engineer.

Investigative (I) types like to work with data, pursuing creative investigation in the scientific area. Careers include biologist, chemist, anthropologist, and medical technologist.

Artistic (A) types work with words, music, or other artistic media. Careers include actor, artist, director, writer, and musician.

Social (S) types like working with others, helping, teaching, or leading. Careers include counselor, nurse, teacher, social worker, and psychologist.

Enterprising (E) types work with other people selling, persuading, and leading. Careers include salesperson, manager, sports promoter, and buyer.

FIGURE 9.5: Enterprising

Conventional (C) types work with data, keep records, and like details and numbers. Careers include bookkeeper, stenographer, financial analyst, and banker.

FIGURE 9.6: Conventional

Strong Interest Inventory and Self-Directed Search

The **Strong Interest Inventory (SII)** is a testing instrument designed to help individuals identify their patterns of interest, and the careers associated with those expressed interests. The philosophical underpinnings of the SII are as follows: (1) what people do is a reflection of their interests, and (2) people with similar interests will be satisfied in like occupations, if their values, knowledge, and abilities are relatively equal.

The SII compares one's interests to other people satisfactorily employed in a range of occupations. That is, if John has the same interests as Joe, and Joe is happy in his career choice, then John, too, would probably be happy in that career. *The SII addresses interests not abilities.*

The **Self-Directed Search (SDS)** was published by John Holland and usually consists of two booklets. One is called the **Assessment Booklet**, which allows individuals taking it to score themselves and get the immediate results. The **Occupations Finder Booklet** shows the Holland combinations and a plethora of occupations that go with them. This booklet also introduces the **DOT**—*Dictionary of Occupational Titles*—which provides more information on each occupation. The SDS may also be taken online.

Individuals may have only one code or a combination of codes that reflect their interests. The interest inventories focus on the **congruence** between the identified Holland Codes and the work environment. For example, if an individual's results show he or she has interests in the artistic (A) and social (S) categories and the individual decides to pursue a career that is primarily represented by the conventional (C) Holland Code—let's say accountant—then this would be **incongruent**. That is, the individual's identified interests **do not match** the interests of happily employed accountants. A better career choice for this individual would be an art teacher, which includes both the artistic and social elements. *Remember, if you cannot find a career that matches your interests, make sure to integrate your interest as a leisure activity.*

Interests and You

You can use the Holland Code results in two ways: (1) to understand how your likes/dislikes fit into the world of work, and (2) to point out areas where your interests differ substantially from those people working in occupations you are considering. Remember, interests represent only one piece of the career decision-making puzzle. When all the pieces are placed together, a truer picture begins to form, and your "right fit" occupational choice will begin to emerge.

The idea of interests ties in with one of Maslow's attributes for self-actualization: greater freshness of appreciation and richness of emotional reaction. Here Maslow states that "the individual will have the capacity, in any given moment, to appreciate the beauty and richness of people and things that they see on a daily basis, and will live in the present moment."

You need to develop the capacity to be interested in many things, and see the value and beauty in a variety of life experiences. It is through the development of your interests that the tapestry of your life is enriched and career paths are chosen.

Values

Man is made by his beliefs.
As he believes, so he is.

—The Bhagavad Gita

Values refer to things a person considers important or desirable. Each of us determines which behaviors, feeling states, or principles are necessary for a satisfying life.

Values vary from person to person. For example, Sam thinks having a lot of money is vital to his life. Sally, on the other hand, lives for love. Values represent the needs that we use to shape our behavior and set goals. Our values are influenced by family, friends, religious affiliation, schools, books, movies, the media, and our life experiences.

Core Values—also known as Personal Values

Values are one of the filters through which we perceive the world, and give meaning to our experiences. Some research suggests that values remain relatively stable over a lifetime. These kinds of values are known as **core values**. Core values are so important and meaningful that they tend to be nonnegotiable. At age nineteen, John valued love, honor, and honesty, and lived his life based on those values. Today, at age forty-nine, John still holds those values close to his heart. What is important to John today will remain so twenty years from now. **Personal, or Core values** are important to us in guiding our lives and in our decision making.

Take notice of a certain movie you watch over and over again. The reason that you are attracted to that movie is that it contains certain core values that resonate within you. For example, extrapolate the core values from the movie "Shawshank Redemption"; friendship, freedom, faith, and hope are just a few. Write down a few a your favorite movies and notice that the same core values appearing.

Internal Compass

Carl Rogers, the humanist psychologist, believed that valuing is a process of self-actualization. It involves choosing freely from alternatives, thinking about their consequences, and prizing and acting on those choices. Our capacity to understand what is desirable and important to us aids in developing our own **internal compass** (internal locus of control) and to rely less on external factors (powerful others, chance control).

Identifying your values directly impacts on decision making. Values form our goals, and goals determine our actions (decisions). If a goal is not based on a truly desired (value-laden) outcome, then there will be insufficient motivation to bring the goal to reality. Here is an example: Sally does not value education. She thinks it is a waste of time at this point in her life, she is only attending college to please her parents. Sally will find out in a very short period of time that she doesn't have the motivation to stay in school and will probably do poorly or drop out before graduation.

Work Values

Work values have to do with how you feel about work; what you need to have reflected in the work environment; and what you want to get out of work. Work values can be categorized as **intrinsic and extrinsic**. Remember, working as a homemaker or working from home will also require looking at your work values, and making sure they match.

Intrinsic work values relate to a specific interest you have in the activities of work, and how you believe the work benefits and contributes to society. Intrinsic values also have to do with the degree to which you are motivated, and satisfied at work on a daily basis. Intrinsic values include the following: variety, helping others, helping society, adventure, risk-taking, influencing others, and achievement.

Extrinsic values relate to the tangible rewards or conditions found at work, as well as earning potential, benefits, and job title. Extrinsic values also involve the physical setting and conditions of the workplace. Extrinsic values include the following: power/authority, money, intellectual status, prestige, flexible work hours, working under pressure, and working in an aesthetically pleasing environment.

Values and Career Decision

Core values, personal values, work values, intrinsic/extrinsic values—what does knowing all of these values have to do with career decision making? Research indicates that when individuals engage in a career that is congruent with their values, they tend to feel more satisfied and are generally more successful in their career. Mary values family, flexible work hours, and leisure time, yet she works as a fledgling lawyer in a prestigious New York law firm that requires her to work a minimum of seventy hours a week. Even with all the hours she puts in at the office, she still takes work home. This scenario reflects the disconnect between Mary's values and her workplace. We can hypothesize that at some point in the very near future, Mary will experience a great deal of stress from this conflict in values. She will be forced to make a decision as to whether she will continue on at the law firm or find a workplace that is congruent with her values.

A person can consider many values to be desirable and important. As cited earlier, we have core values or personal values, and work values. Some core or personal values can be met in the workplace; others cannot. Values need to be prioritized so that the influences of each do not compete, but work together in a coherent pattern, like a patchwork quilt. Knowing your values will facilitate self-understanding and make decision making easier for you.

Values and You

Clarifying your values will enhance self-awareness; help you to make better ethical decisions; develop greater integrity because your stated values will match your actions; improve your ability to prioritize; and assist you in making a better "career fit" choice.

We can align values with another of Maslow's attributes for self-actualization: certain changes in the value system. Values for self-actualizing individuals are more for others than self. Self-actualized individuals aspire to such values as beauty, love, altruism, and spirituality. Values for individuals who have not yet reached self-actualization would be those values that have their root in necessity. Those in the survival mode would have such values as safety, money, security, and conformity.

Maslow contends that "you will have an acceptance of the nature of self, human nature, social life, nature, and physical reality. Values will become universal, and centered on the good of others, rather than for the good of self."

Reflective FOCUS

▼ Although your personality type plays an extremely important role in your career choice, what role do your interests and values play in your career choice?

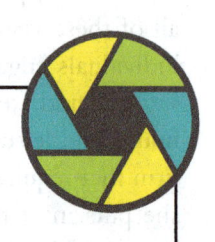

PART IV

Finding Your Bliss

Image © SHS Photography, 2014. Used under license from Shutterstock, Inc.

Having made the decision to go home, Odysseus builds a ship and designs an escape plan. He returns home and the goddess Athena turns him into an old beggar (stripped of all his worldly possessions and social status) so he can determine if his wife still wants him after 20 years. He wins back his wife and is transformed into his natural self. He has finally found his bliss.

The journey thus far has revealed many hidden aspects of your inner self that may have obscured your ability to identify your "bliss." You are now equipped with the tools to label your bliss, but the journey does not end here. You will now be tasked with marrying the knowledge you have gained about yourself to the components that are essential to helping you with the challenges of finding your bliss. Therefore, the next part of the journey focuses on critical thinking, decision making, mind, body, and spirit.

chapter 10
Thinking Clearly

CRITICAL THINKING AND DECISION MAKING

"Each problem that I solved became a rule which served afterwards to solve other problems."

–Rene Descartes

"Most people would sooner die than think; in fact, they do so."

–Bertrand Russell

Image © Sergey Nivens, 2014. Used under license from Shutterstock, Inc.

Reading, writing, and arithmetic have been the three traditional pillars of American education. With the advent of the twenty-first century, a fourth pillar, critical thinking, needs to be added to the existing educational foundation.

As college and university graduates enter the workforce, it is essential that they possess strong critical-thinking skills as well as training for their chosen field. Employers in the twenty-first century require that their prospective employees display basic employability skills; chief among these is the ability to think critically.

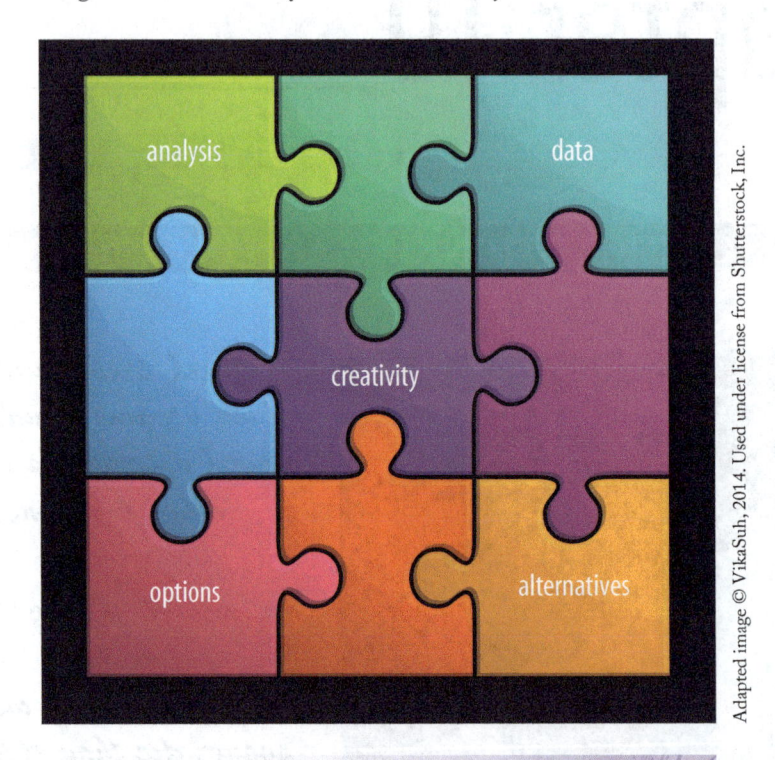

FIGURE 10.1: Critical thinking is like putting together a puzzle; you need to make sure each piece is the right one for your picture.

What Is Critical Thinking?

One definition states:

> *Critical thinking is the intellectually disciplined process of actively and skillfully, conceptualizing, applying, analyzing, synthesizing, and/or evaluating information gathered from, or generated by, observation, experience, reflection, reasoning, or communication, as a guide to belief and action.*

(Scriven and Paul, 1996)

PART IV: Finding Your Bliss

In simpler terms, critical thinking is the art of reasoned judgment, or how the individual uses the thought process in making decisions, or forming evaluations about various aspects of his or her life. Does the individual go about life accepting whatever others say or do? Or does the individual analyze, evaluate, discriminate, and use reason to make his or her own choices and judgments?

Critical thinking is a process that assists the individual in evaluating ideas and information, and the sources from which they originate; arranging the ideas and information in a logical, coherent manner; making connections to other ideas and information; and generating alternatives. In other words, if people are critical thinkers, they do not accept things at face value; they look below the surface of the information that is being presented, and arrive at their own conclusions and beliefs.

Critical thinking is not a skill reserved for the classroom. The intellectual skills of critical thinking are not only needed by college graduates. All of us, from grocer and waitress to engineer and fashion designer need to have good thinking and reasoning skills. In every aspect of our lives we will be called upon to make decisions and choices which the outcomes will be, in many cases, the direct result of the quality of our critical thinking ability. When a woman shops and tries to determine whether she will save money by buying Brand X or Brand Y, she is engaged in critical thinking. A young man buying his first car, and trying to decide whether a Toyota or a Honda will give him better gas mileage, is using critical-thinking skills. Both of these examples represent one end of the continuum of critical thinking; as you become skilled in this kind of thinking, you develop a more sophisticated ability to reason and think in alternative ways (i.e., "think out of the box").

Characteristics of Critical Thinkers

Critical thinking is a skill that can be learned. The underlying premise of the process is that individuals are responsible for their own thinking. A good critical thinker has the ability to:

- use reason and logic;
- understand context;
- evaluate;
- grasp principles;
- hypothesize (assuming probable outcomes based on existing criteria);

FIGURE 10.2

- classify;
- offer opinions with reason;
- make judgments with criteria; and
- use clear communication.

Barriers to Critical Thinking

There are a number of obstacles that can interfere with an individual becoming a skilled critical thinker. The nature of the obstacles can be perceptual, emotional, cultural, environmental, or intellectual and expressive.

Perceptual obstacles can interfere with how a problem is first perceived. They include the following: stereotyping, difficulty in isolating the problem, inability to see the problem from various viewpoints, and failure to use all of one's senses.

Emotional obstacles influence and limit how one sees and thinks about a problem. Examples include fear of taking a risk, discomfort with chaos, and judging rather than creating ideas.

Your **cultural background** can also limit how you look at potential problems. If your cultural upbringing doesn't place any value on fantasy and reflection (two necessary elements of critical and creative thinking), then you aren't likely to engage in those behaviors. Some cultures place high value on reason, logic, numbers, and practicality; they see feeling, intuition, and qualitative judgments as useless. Both of these biases, if unexamined, will derail the process of good critical thinking.

Environmental obstacles to critical thinking are the lack of cooperation and trust among colleagues; an autocratic boss who only values his or her own ideas; distractions and lack of support for new ideas. People are not generally willing to put forth new and different solutions if they feel their coworkers or supervisors are not open to accepting those ideas. Environmental obstacles can also take the form of family members. Some parents resist having their children think for themselves. Parents often want their children to accept their beliefs, opinions, and ideas without questioning them. At times, parents do the thinking for their children in an effort to make things easier for them. In the college setting, parents will often come with their children to freshman orientation and answer all the questions the advisor directs toward the student. When this happens, students rarely get the opportunity to voice their preferences, or learn how to interact with the advisor on an adult level.

Intellectual and expressive obstacles are created when individuals display the inability to (a) convey information accurately or adequately, and (b) clearly express themselves verbally.

Ways to Develop Critical Thinking

One of the ways to develop critical-thinking skills is to use the steps to rational decision making on a daily basis to resolve problems large and small. When faced with any potential decision: (1) pinpoint the problem, (2) gather data, (3) analyze data, (4) determine alternatives, (5) evaluate consequences, (6) imagine paying the consequences, (7) choose, (8) act, and (9) evaluate.

Critical Thinking and You

The brain loves to learn and think. From a biological perspective, the brain learns to solve problems in order to advance its chances of survival. The best thing you can do from the brain's point of view is to think, think, think!

One of Maslow's attributes of self-actualization, "superior perception of reality," aligns well with critical thinking. He states that individuals will have an efficient perception of reality. They will have an exceptional ability to reason.

A person with good critical-thinking skills tends to be healthier and more secure. They are able to accurately discern the motivations and behaviors of others, detect dishonesty, and generally judge people correctly. This ability allows an individual to operate from a position of reason rather than anxiety or fear.

Perceiving the world accurately, having good judgment, being able to think "out of the conventional box," and thinking logically are all attributes of good critical thinkers.

Decision Making

The process of living life is really one of daily decision making; every morning you get up and decide what to wear, what to eat, and how you feel. The decisions are large and small. Choosing a career is just another decision in a long line of decisions. However, it is a decision that most of us rank high in importance, yet one that many of us think will be resolved magically.

A good decision-maker has the ability to look at the big picture, identify his or her values, and understand the larger impact of any decision.

Your values are an indication of what is of primary importance to you. Knowing your values allows for the use of that information as a framework for future decisions. The reality is that you will only be motivated to act on a decision if that decision aligns in a positive way with what you consider important.

Though decision making seems like a simple process, many of us have a great deal of difficulty making decisions. There are a number of things that can impact your ability to make choices. One is related to your Myers-Briggs Type Indicator.

In the section on the MBTI, we talked about people having a preference for feeling or thinking. The functions of feeling and thinking have to do with how people prefer to make decisions.

Feelers like to take into account their feelings and emotions, as well as other people's feelings when they make a decision. Feelers prefer harmony over clarity. Often feelers will avoid making a decision, because they worry that conflict will be the result. **Thinkers** make their decisions based on facts and logic. Feelings and emotions are only data to be weighed in a choice, but not essential to the process. Thinkers do not mind making difficult decisions, and they do not understand why others get upset about issues that are not relevant to the decision being made.

Other reasons that sometimes make it difficult for people to make decisions have to do with the biochemistry of **emotions, emotional intelligence**, and **self-esteem**.

Emotions and Self-Esteem

If you have low self-esteem, and have issues of abandonment and rejection, it can be very difficult to make a good, rational decision. Often, when people don't feel "good enough" about themselves, they can get stuck in their emotions and unconsciously do things to reject themselves. These factors include repression, resistance, drama, acting out, worry, guilt, being overly emotional, judging, and controlling. These behaviors are a form of self-sabotage, and can prevent a person from making healthy, growth-enhancing choices.

How do you get out of your own way if you are someone who has trouble making decisions? For one, you can assess your level of self-esteem and if it is low, learn ways to enhance your confidence (see the section on self-esteem). Next, look at whether you have appropriate levels of emotional intelligence. Remember, it is not enough to have a high IQ and be a brilliant thinker. You need to know how to negotiate the real world of people and relationships (see the section on emotional intelligence). Finally, realize that decision making is really a matter of making one choice over another. Even if you have made bad choices in the past, you can learn from those experiences and make better choices now.

Career decision making is subject to the same process of rational thinking as any other decision. Because it is a process of thinking, anyone can learn the skill and become a good problem solver/decision-maker.

Process of Rational Decision Making

The process of rational decision making begins with realizing that you need to do something about a situation you are facing. Once you are committed to solving a problem, you can begin to employ the steps of rational thinking.

STEP 1: Pinpoint the problem. What is it you want to accomplish?

STEP 2: Gather data. What information do you need to help you accomplish your goal?

STEP 3: Analyze the data. Is the information good? Do you need to gather more information?

STEP 4: Generate alternatives. What options do you have? Have you brainstormed all the possibilities? Are there unacceptable alternatives?

STEP 5: Evaluate the alternatives. What are the possible outcomes of each alternative action? How much risk am I willing to take?

STEP 6: Choose and act. Select from the alternatives you have generated and take action.

STEP 7: Evaluate the choice/action. How well is my choice working? Did unexpected things happen? Am I flexible enough to revise my plans to make them work better?

Decision Making and You

In becoming familiar with the process of rational thinking, your decision-making skill will progressively improve. Therefore, instead of being immobilized when faced with making momentous decisions, you will be able to face any situation with greater confidence and less anxiety.

REFERENCES AND RECOMMENDED READINGS:

Andolina, M. (2002). *Practical Guide to Critical Thinking*. Albany, NY: Delmar-Thomson Learning.

Hughes, W. (1996). *Critical Thinking: An Introduction to Basic Skills*. Peterborough, ON: Broadview Press.

Jensen, E. (1996). *Brain-based Learning*. Del Mar, CA: Turning Point Publishing.

Scriven, M., & Paul, R. (1996). Defining critical thinking: A draft statement for the National Council for Excellence in Critical Thinking [on-line]. Available http://www.criticalthinking.org/University/univlibrary/library.nclk

Reflective FOCUS

▼ How does asking the "right questions" help you to become a successful critical thinker?

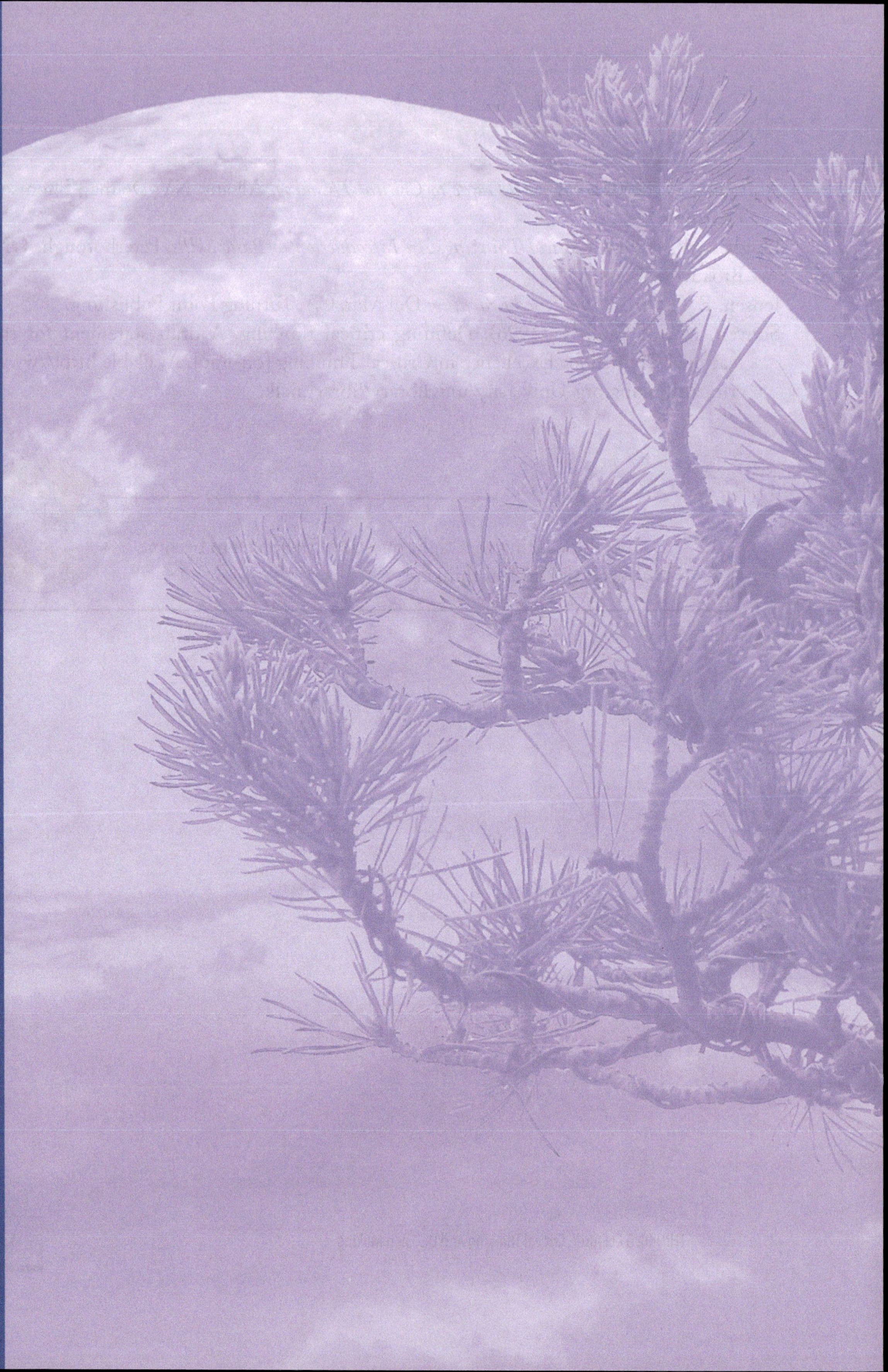

chapter 11

The Integrated You

MIND, BODY, AND SPIRIT

"If your spiritual philosophy is not moving you to the state of peace, health, wealth and love your spirit desires . . . you need a new spiritual philosophy."

–Sun Bear

Image © Jackiso, 2014. Used under license from Shutterstock, Inc.

This section will focus on the interconnectedness of mind, body, and spirit. Although they are separate in nature, they do not operate independently of each other.

Carl Jung hypothesized that if individuals do not follow their **"soul's blueprint,"** that is, the life path they are meant to follow (i.e., their bliss), over time physical ailments will manifest. Jung felt that fulfilling your soul's blueprint is essential for a healthy mind, body, and spirit. The following case study illustrates how the body reacts to the stresses of the mind and spirit.

Jake is an ENFP (extravert, intuitive, feeling, perceiving) who always wanted to go into graphic design. Unfortunately, he felt the only jobs he could get were in computer programming, so he took a job as a programmer. Jake was bothered by the routine and tedious nature of the job. He had to work mostly alone, and by the end of the day, he would be drained of energy. The routine and detailed work goes against Jake's intuitive and perceiving nature, and lack of human contact goes against his extravert preference. He felt stifled in his creativity and began calling off work, more and more frequently, due to colds and the flu. He eventually quit the job and found one in graphic design. His frustration and inability to fulfill his passion troubled his spirit which in turn caused the physical ailments. As he followed his bliss, his physical symptoms disappeared.

In addition to the soul's blueprint, other factors can contribute to an unhealthy mind, body, and spirit. The **four most toxic factors** are **anger, criticism, resentment,** and **guilt.**

Deepak Chopra

Present-day health guru Deepak Chopra says a person's body ages and decays because of his or her preconceived beliefs of time, and the separate nature of the body and mind. He states:

> *Our cells are constantly eavesdropping on our thoughts and being changed by them. A bout of depression can wreak havoc with the immune system; falling in love can boost it. Despair and hopelessness raise the risk of heart attacks and cancer, thereby shortening life. Joy and fulfillment keep us healthy and extend life. This means that the line between biology and psychology can't really be drawn with any certainty. A remembered stress, which is only a wisp of thought, releases the same flood of destructive hormones as the stress itself (Chopra, 1999).*
>
> Excerpt(s) from *Ageless Body, Timeless Mind: The Quantum Alternative to Growing Old* by Deepak Chopra, M.D., copyright © 1993 by Deepak Chopra. Used by permission of Harmony Books, an imprint of the Crown Publishing Group, a division of Random House LLC. All rights reserved. Any third party use of this material, outside of this publication, is prohibited. Interested parties must apply directly to Random House LLC for permission.

Based on Chopra's views, we need to:

- Recognize that the mind and body are one.
- Realize that beliefs, thoughts, and emotions create the chemical reaction that upholds life in every cell.

The Mind

We have already seen, in the chapter on emotional intelligence, how our emotions and thoughts create corresponding chemical changes in our body when we habitually express an emotion. And in the chapter on social intelligence, we have seen that our brains are wired for social connectedness with other people.

Scientists are continuing to do research on the mind's ability to facilitate healing of the body to try and identify the exact mechanisms within the brain that can account for this phenomenon. There are many anecdotal stories of people being told by their doctors that they have six months to live and yet they beat the odds to live for another ten years.

Let's look at some of the things you can do to have a healthier mind.

We discussed the power our thoughts and our words have on us and others in the chapter on self-empowerment. So you can begin to have a healthier mind by looking at your thoughts and recognizing what cognitive therapists call "cognitive distortions" in your thinking.

Here are some common examples of cognitive distortions:

- All-or-nothing thinking ("If I don't get this job, I'll never apply for another job in this field again")
- Overgeneralization ("I had a terrible relationship with a Greek man, therefore, all Greek men stink")
- Rejection of the positive (seeing the glass half empty, instead of half full)
- Mind reading ("I just know that person thinks I am an idiot")
- Everything is a catastrophe ("I failed the test; it's the worst thing that could ever happen to me")
- Should statements ("I should have applied for that job yesterday")

CHAPTER 11: THE INTEGRATED YOU: Mind, Body, and Spirit

After recognizing the cognitive distortions in your thinking, cognitive reconstruction can begin. **Cognitive reconstruction** is the act of replacing negative thoughts and emotions with positive ones. This practice is something that requires patience and perseverance because some of the distortions have been around for a while, and will not go away overnight.

Intuition

Intuition is another aspect of the mind/brain to develop to help you in your life. Is intuition *hocus pocus* or a viable tool to use in planning one's life and career path? The authors devoted a section in this chapter to the discussion of intuition because the idea of listening to one's inner voice, discovering the hidden self, and acknowledging the promptings of the subconscious; are all essential to Joseph Campbell's concept of "finding one's bliss." All of these are vehicles through which intuition imparts information to the individual.

The word *intuition* comes from the Latin, "intueri" which means to look into. *Webster's Dictionary* defines intuition as "an immediate knowing or learning of something without the conscious use of reasoning." To understand and accept intuition, one needs to leave behind the notion of traditional logic, and move into the realm of symbols, signs, and nonlinear thinking.

BRAIN-BASED PERSPECTIVE

From a brain-based perspective, intuition finds a home in the workings of the right brain. The right brain is holistic, imaginistic, processes symbols and complex images, and sees things in relation to other things. The left brain is logical, linear, analytic, and compartmentalized. Intuition clearly flies in the face of the left brain's domain. Yet, once "intuition" reaches consciousness, it is the left brain's skills that can support and bring to realization an intuitive idea (as in rational decision making).

Neuroscientists conducting current research on intuition believe that the ventromedial prefrontal cortex of the brain might be involved in emotions and decision making (Antonio Damasio, University of Iowa) and that this area of the brain is responsible for intuition. They hypothesize that intuition is a result of the unconscious and instantaneous processing of data and emotions that may be stored in this area of the brain. So that when you have an "AHA" moment it is not really a mystical thing but the brain's incredible ability to process and connect the stored information from your experiences. There is still more research to be done but this research supports the idea that everyone (barring brain injury to this portion of the prefrontal cortex) has the capacity for intuition.

In the meantime, while we are waiting for scientists to give us the definitive word on the matter, we can begin to develop or key into our intuitions, which allows us to tap into our own inner wisdom; become present to the moment; unlock the inner guide; develop self-trust and self-confidence; and come to the realization that answers are available to us at every moment.

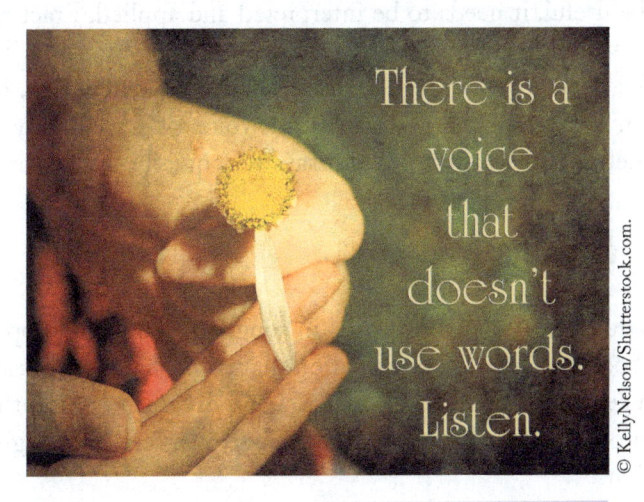

FIGURE 11.1

WHAT DOES INTUITION LOOK LIKE?

Intuition can take many forms. It can be:

- a "gut feeling" that something is good or bad;
- signs and symbols that speak to the individual;
- a flash of inspiration—the "aha" moment;
- the ability to visualize a future event;
- a "little voice" that speaks in warning;
- dreams that deliver important messages;
- a persistent yearning to pursue something different;
- a sense of deja vu; or
- a synchronistic event (similar things occurring at the same time without any direct link between the two).

DEVELOPING INTUITION

How does one begin to develop intuition? Developing intuition is an unsettling proposition at first because it is difficult to discern intuition from the normal thinking process. One suggestion is to keep an intuition journal where you can "log in" an intuitive thought as it is received. Intuitions come to individuals through a variety of avenues. They can be very subtle, symbolic, and abstract, or they can rise up like an elephant in the living room.

For intuition to be useful, it needs to be interpreted and applied. Practicing, trusting, and acting on intuitions quickly is another way to further develop intuition. The rule of thumb is, if one feels the need to second-guess the information coming in, it is probably **not** intuition. Intuition is not the excited, worried little voice saying, "Oh my gosh, we're gonna hit that car and die!" It is the little voice that says very quietly, "Pull over now."

HOW TO RECOGNIZE INTUITION

Intuitive information can come from words in songs that suddenly pop out and resonate with meaning; a book with needed information that coincidentally appears on the desk; or the messages in a person's dreams. Individuals can use **dreams** to access their inner wisdom to resolve a career or life issue. The unconscious mind is at its best at night, when there are no other distractions.

Carl Jung, in his memoir, *Memories, Dreams, and Reflections*, said that he received his ideas and information about his theory of personality development from visionary guides, synchronistic events, and telepathic experiences. In other words, he accessed his intuition to create an original psychological theory.

History is filled with people who have been inspired by their intuitions. Leonardo da Vinci's early prototypes for the camera and flying machine were prophetic visions of things to come. Jules Verne's book, *Mysterious Island*, written in the early 1800s, describes with surprising accuracy the modern submarine. Jonas Salk, who discovered penicillin, writes, "It is always with excitement that I wake up in the morning wondering what my intuitor will toss up to me like gifts from the sea." One can speculate that perhaps the Microsoft phenomenon is a product of Bill Gates's intuitive mind.

Where would civilization be if people had closed themselves off to the inner whisperings that showed them the path they were meant to travel in their lives? Would man have ever set foot on the moon? Or would a man in New York be communicating via the Internet with a woman in Tokyo?

Intuition and You

In conjunction with reason and emotion, intuition can be a valuable tool for you to use to navigate life's journey. Most of all, remember to "be still and listen."

The Body

Years ago, there was an episode of the original *Star Trek* television series in which an alien species, who were pure energy and no longer had corporeal form, took over the bodies of Kirk, Spock, and McCoy. The first words out of the mouths of these aliens upon inhabiting the human body referenced how amazing it was to be back in a physical body and to have sensations.

We humans take our bodies for granted. We often forget how truly incredible is the design of the human body. We overeat and drink. We don't exercise enough, or we pound our joints with Zumba classes, racquetball, marathon running, and aerobics.

There is an epidemic of obesity in the country. Younger and younger people are having knee and hip replacements. Acid reflux is on the rise.

If we want to have healthy bodies, many of us need to change our habits. Research on people who live long and healthy lives shows that proper nutrition and exercise are the foundation for long-term health.

EXERCISE

FIGURE 11.2

FIGURE 11.3

FIGURE 11.4

There are various types of exercises, and one should find the best exercise to fit his or her individual needs. Research shows that exercise has a positive impact on mood by raising endorphin levels in the body. It can raise HDL levels in the blood and increase lung capacity. Aerobics, weight training, swimming, jogging, and walking are popular methods of exercise. If individuals have problems with their joints then they need to participate in low-impact forms of exercise. There is an old adage in relation to exercise: "Use it or lose it."

For activities that calm the spirit while strengthening the body, try the following:

- **Hatha Yoga,** from ancient India. Focus is on breathing and a series of physical postures that result in better overall health.

PART IV: Finding Your Bliss

- **Tai Chi,** from ancient China. Focus is on precision movement and breathing that develop balance, control, and relaxation.
- **Massage Therapy,** including Swedish, neuromuscular, deep tissue, and aromatherapy; assists the body with circulation, releases muscle tension, promotes relaxation, and reduces stress.

DIET AND NUTRITION

The United States Department of Agriculture (USDA) has updated its food pyramid to reflect the latest studies on human nutrition. More emphasis has been placed on fruits, grains, pastas, cereals, and vegetables, and less on dairy products and meats. Studies have shown that diets high in fat and calories lead to chronic disease and morbidity. Conversely, diets rich in fiber, fruits, and vegetables reduce obesity and lower the risk of heart disease and cancer.

Research done on longevity supports the idea of eating smaller portions. Restaurants in the United States are beginning to get on board with this concept by offering "lighter options" and/or choice of plate size.

The Spirit

It is difficult to define "*spirit*." Spirit is different for each person and culture or religion. For purposes of this book, we define spirit as that intangible aspect of ourselves that yearns for centeredness, joy, peace, and a life of meaning.

There are a variety of methods that help lift the spirit. Relaxation exercises have been clinically proven to reduce stress and create a sense of calm and tranquility.

- **Progressive Muscle Relaxation.**
  The goal of this type of relaxation is to relax all your muscles from head to toes in a systematic way. As with most relaxation exercises, this one begins by either sitting or lying down in a comfortable position, with eyes open or shut. Slowly inhale and exhale and begin to focus on your breathing. Starting with your head and moving down to your feet, begin to tense and relax each muscle in your body. Then reverse the procedure and go from your feet, back to your head. Your body will be completely relaxed and all the muscles loose.

- **Hypnosis** is more than a parlor trick used at sideshows to embarrass and entertain audiences. The goal of hypnosis is to plant suggestions for your benefit in your subconscious mind that you will implement in your conscious state. It's a valuable method to use for smoking cessation, weight loss, pain management, and personal counseling. One of the benefits of hypnosis is the wonderful calm feeling experienced at the end of the session. Hypnosis also assists in eliminating bad habits, panic attacks, nightmares, and general and localized anxiety. Using a certified hypnotherapist is recommended.

- **Meditation.** The goal of meditation is to slow down the *"monkey mind"* or constant chatter that goes on in one's mind so that the mind can become calmer. Some forms of meditation include transcendental meditation, walking meditations, mindfulness meditation, imagery, and subject matter meditations such as, love, forgiveness, and peace. Meditation, in all of its forms, can lead to a peaceful, relaxed state. Find a quiet place and either sit or lie down in a comfortable position, with eyes open or shut. Begin to focus on each breath as you slowly inhale and exhale. Concentrate on something specific such as an affirmation, a word, a feeling, a person, or a beautiful picture in your mind. Continue the meditation for at least five minutes. Over time, it will be easier to concentrate for longer periods of time. Meditating at least three times a week has been proven to boost the immune system, improve digestion, sharpen thinking skills, and promote an overall feeling of well-being.

- **Prayer.** Regardless of one's religious or spiritual belief, prayer is an effective method for healing the spirit. There is no right or wrong way to pray. For every religion or spiritual belief, there are just as many methods of prayer.

Embracing Joy

"Joy, beautiful, divine spark" . . . this is a line from a poem that inspired Beethoven in 1824 to compose the "Ode to Joy" as part of his Ninth Symphony. When one hears the symphony, the listener is transported by the sublime music to exalted heights . . . to feelings of, well, joy!

Abraham Maslow addressed joy in his eighth attribute: "Higher frequency of peak experiences. The individual will have feelings of limitless horizons opening up to the vision, the feeling of being simultaneously more powerful and also more helpless than one ever was before, the feeling of ecstasy and wonder and awe, the loss of placement in time and space with, finally, the conviction that something extremely important and valuable has happened, so that the subject was to some extent transformed and strengthened even in his daily life by such experiences." (Maslow, 1968)

This could be the most elusive of Maslow's self-actualization attributes. Who would not want to experience "the feeling of ecstasy and wonder and awe" and the "loss of placement in time and space"? We can only hope that when we find our bliss, whether that is a certain career path, providing a good home, or both—we will have moments of such transformation that everything else will fall into place; and our own existence will be a healthier, happier, and a more pleasant place to be.

A recent *New York Times* article commented on the fact that so many college students on campuses across the United States are joyless. That is, they are so stressed by school, selecting majors, choosing careers, juggling jobs and families, and worrying about the future, that they walk around in states of unhappiness and depression. This situation has become of such concern on some campuses that college administrators have brought massage therapists on campus to offer biofeedback workshops.

Joy is an emotion that transcends happiness. It is a feeling of gladness that incorporates both meaning and gratefulness. What brings joy is unique to each individual; for some, joy is seeing a beautiful sunset, and for others it is playing with their Labrador puppy.

Several factors contribute to one's ability to experience joy: high self-esteem, being optimistic, and having a sense of personal control (internal locus of control). It also helps to have close relationships that provide support, to be engaged in both work and leisure activities, and to have a sense of meaning and purpose in one's life.

The goal for you is to discover the things, people, and experiences that bring you joy, and then to cultivate and nourish what has been discovered.

FIGURE 11.5: Joyful

Mind, Body, Spirit, and You

It is important for you to recognize the interconnectedness of the mind, body, and spirit. Every thought (and deed) has either a positive, negative, or neutral affect on the body and spirit. You cannot hate and expect to live in peace. The lesson is easy, but the homework is tough. It's all about making the right choices, standing by them, and being consistent in your practice.

May the road rise to meet you.
May the wind be always at your back.
May the sun shine warm upon your face,
And the rains fall short upon your fields.
And until we meet again,
May God hold you in the palm of his hand.

—Old Irish Blessing

REFERENCES AND RECOMMENDED READINGS:

Cassileth, B.R. (1998). *The Alternative Medicine Handbook*. New York: Norton.
Chopra, D. (1993). *Ageless Body, Timeless Mind*. New York: Harmony Books.
Damasio, A. (1997). The brains behind intuition. *Science* [online]. http//:news.sciencemag.org/1997/brains-behind-intuition.
Goleman, D., & Gurin, J. (Eds.) (1996). *Mind Body Medicine*. New York: Consumer Report Books.
Hay, L.L. (1988). *Heal Your Body*. Carlsbad, CA: Hay House Inc.
Maslow, A. (1968). *Toward a Psychology of Being*. New York: Van Nostrand Reinhold.

Reflective FOCUS

▼ What would bring joy to your life?

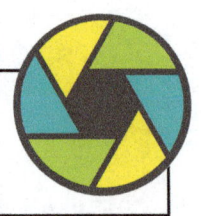

chapter 12
The Journey's End

Photo by Scott Kelly.

"Twenty years from now you will be more disappointed by the things that you didn't do than by the ones you did do. So throw off the bowlines. Sail away from the safe harbor. Catch the trade winds in your sails. Explore. Dream. Discover."

—H. Jackson Brown Jr.

It appears that the journey is over, but it has really just begun. Like Odysseus (the hero), you are on your own journey. When you metaphorically "**left home**" in order to start of new life, several key issues appeared: (a) you searched for the meaning of life and the motivation you needed to obtain your bliss, (b) you discovered your place on Maslow's Hierarchy of Needs, and (c) you explored the wonderful attributes to which you could aspire as part of self-actualization.

Through "**trials and tribulations,**" you discovered the limitations of having an external locus of control, the benefits of having an internal locus of control, and you learned to rely on your own power. During this time of trials and tribulations, you also looked at your own

135

level of self-esteem; discovering how it had impacted your life and choices, and you created ways to develop a stronger sense of self and a positive outlook.

As you became aware of your emotional intelligence quotient (EQ), and the challenges associated with a low EQ, you began to understand how handling emotions inappropriately could hinder the attainment of your bliss. You have learned to understand how social intelligence impacts your relationships with others, and how your perception of diversity could impact your place in society.

With the use of assessments, you "**looked within**" to uncover your personality preferences, interests, and values. Your personality type and interests results shed light on the relationship of personality type and career choice, as well as interpersonal relationships. You discovered what was important to you through identifying your personal and work values. In order to find the right "fit" career, you realized that you must look at all three components—personality, interests, and values—and understand how they interrelate to determine the path that supports your passion.

The journey thus far has revealed many hidden aspects of inner self that may have obscured your ability to identify your "**bliss**." You now realize that the common thread throughout your journey is the understanding that mind, body, and spirit are all connected, and need to be kept in balance if you are to find lasting bliss. However, the journey does not end here; you must discover the means to attain your "bliss." This stage will help you discover those

FIGURE 12.1

PART IV: Finding Your Bliss

means by requiring you to apply the critical-thinking, decision-making, and intuition skills that you have gained.

In traveling the path to "bliss," you may encounter intangible elements that may delay the attainment of your passion. Just as Odysseus was tempted by the Siren's song, and his hubris angered the gods and incurred their wrath, your own fears or lack of courage, trust, and faith can turn you away from your destined path.

How do you maintain courage in the face of outside influences that continually dictate how you should live your life? How do you close your ears to the cacophony of society's opinions about who and what you should be? Begin by having an "attitude of gratitude" and being grateful for what you have and envision what you would like to have in the future. Though it can be challenging to do, maintaining a positive outlook can be enormously helpful to you on your journey. Research shows that positivity triggers the area of the brain that activates opiates and dopamine to be released. Scientists believe that dopamine may help our drive and persistence while the opiates increase our feelings of pleasure. Talking about your goals and what you envision for yourself in the future in a positive way can trigger your brain centers to release these feel good chemicals which in turn help to open you up to new possibilities. **Remember, the answer lies in having the courage to push past your fears, and find the faith to trust yourself and the path you must walk.**

As you travel on your hero's journey, expect to be lonely at times, to be challenged by others, and, perhaps, to have financial rewards come slowly. However, if you stay the course, you can achieve what Carl Jung called "fulfilling the soul's blueprint." You will be living the life of a self-actualized person, with the ability to have peak experiences, to appreciate beauty and nature to its fullest, to accept others as they are, and to accept yourself unconditionally.

In closing we leave you with a few quotes from Joseph Campbell:

> *"We must be willing to get rid of the life we planned, so as to have the life that is waiting for us. The old skin must be shed before the new one can come."*

> *"When you follow your bliss, doors will open where you would not have thought there would be doors, and where there wouldn't be a door for anyone else."*

STEPS TO THE HERO'S JOURNEY CAREER EXPLORATION PROCESS

Part I. Leaving Home

- **Create Your Dream**: fantasize, imagine, then focus.

Part II. Trials and Tribulations

- **Keep Your Spirits Up**: seek out supportive people, avoid negativism.
- **Don't Overwhelm Yourself**: take time to move through each level of process.
- **Don't Take Rejection/Failure Personally**: learn from setbacks, make adjustments, reassess and try again.

Part III. Looking Within

- **Soul Search**: look inward, reassess, commit.
- **Be Realistic**: take stock of yourself and know what is within the realm of possibility for yourself at the present time.

Part IV. Finding Your Bliss

- **Ask Questions**: seek out information, find mentors, make connections.
- **Read, Study, Learn**: gather as much information as possible regarding your goal/dream.
- **Be Prepared**: do your research, make plans, and strike when opportunity presents itself; make your own luck.
- **Take Action**: be willing to initiate an action to turn your dreams into reality.
- **Listen to Your Intuition**: keep yourself open to possibilities; trust your gut.
- **Design Your Dream to Fit Who You Are.**
- **Persistence**: don't give up; whatever you want, "Go For It!" It *can* happen.
- **Have Patience**: timing is everything!

appendix

RÉSUMÉ/COVER LETTERS/INTERVIEWING PROCESS

The word résumé comes from the French word for "summary," and represents an overview of your work history and skills. Other words that are synonymous with résumé are *personal data sheet* and *curriculum vitae*.

The résumé is the primary sales tool in your search for a job. It is an employer's first introduction to you, and as such, it can be a valuable asset or detriment. An advantage of constructing your own résumé is that it allows you to present yourself in your own way. Farming out the construction of your résumé to another person is not recommended.

The résumé states your qualifications for the job, and serves as the gateway to obtain a job interview. It reveals several important things about job seekers:

- The quality of their communication skills
- Their ability to organize written information in a clear and concise manner
- How well prepared and serious they are about applying for the position
- Whether they have the required skills and qualifications for the desired position

Types of Résumés

There are three common types of résumé:

1. Functional
2. Chronological
3. Combination of Chronological and Functional

The résumé format you select should be the one that does the best job marketing you for the position of interest.

Functional Résumé

The functional résumé shows the candidate's work history, organized around specific functional areas, such as computer programming, software development, marketing, sales, and accounting experience. This format is useful in highlighting work experience that is specifically related to the position being sought. It places less emphasis on dates and locations.

The functional format can be more difficult for employers to use when doing a quick scan to identify key points of information that tell where the candidate has been, what the candidate has been doing, and what professional growth the candidate has experienced through recent job changes. It can also be viewed suspiciously as a means of camouflaging gaps in work history or the lack of a stable work experience.

Chronological Résumé

The chronological résumé is probably the easiest to write for the candidate, and the most commonly accepted form of résumé presentation. In this format, education and work history are listed in reverse chronological order. This format showcases your career growth. However, if you are a new graduate, chronological résumés can send the message that the you lack specific career-related experience.

The Combination Chronological/Functional Résumé

The combination chronological/functional résumé is becoming the format preferred by most people. It combines the best features of both, providing the strongest possible presentation of your skills and abilities, while displaying your historical information (i.e., dates and locations of experience and education). The combination résumé type consists of six basic components:

- Contact Information
- Objective
- Professional Qualifications
- Education
- Work History
- Community Service/Professional Affiliations/Accomplishments

The combination résumé leads with contact information, then the objective; professional qualifications and education can be reversed depending on the skills and experience of the job seeker. You always want to lead with information that presents your strengths, not your limitations.

Structure of a Résumé

In general, the content within the résumé framework should be easy to scan for quick location of information. You want to make it as easy as possible for the prospective employer to see your skills and experience.

- Headings should stand out slightly to the left making it easy for the eye to find.
- Time frames should be aligned at the right margin.
- Visual clues in the design of the format allows the reader to quickly determine:
   (1) the length of employment at each job;
   (2) how often you change jobs (i.e., if you are a job hopper);
   (3) if there are any unaccountable gaps in employment; and
   (4) whether you have been moving up the career ladder.

APPENDIX: Résumé/Cover Letters/Interviewing Process

Education and Employment or Work History are the chronological portions of the combination résumé. Information in these sections should be presented in reverse chronological order, and be visually organized in an identical fashion. It is not necessary to share your complete work and education history on the résumé. Jobs from long ago that are totally irrelevant to your current career focus should not be on a current résumé.

If you have been working for a long time, you may want to provide **only the last ten years** of your work and/or education experiences. This is particularly the case if you are a "mature" job seeker. Irrelevant jobs, and jobs from over ten years ago, should only be listed on the application.

Be careful that your résumé does not leave unaccountable gaps in employment. This is a **"negative flag"** to job recruiters. In addition, citing that you have attended several colleges without completing a degree program might lead an employer to assume that you do not have the ability to follow through, or lack the necessary focus, to complete a project.

Communicate accomplishments in your educational information that relate to the job for which you are applying. If you are currently enrolled in an academic program, list that information.

What Employers Like to See on Résumé

- Quantitative data (that which can be numbered or measured) whenever possible
- Honest and accurate information
- Neat, organized information
- Correct grammar and spelling
- Visually appealing and easy to read format (e.g., use of bullets and bold headings)

Do's and Don'ts of Résumé Writing

DO'S

- Type your résumé on 8 1/2" by 11" good quality bond paper (use white, off-white, cream, or a very light gray, with matching envelopes, if possible) with readable type size – 10 pt. to 12 pt. font.
- Be attentive to the content and visual appearance of your resume.
- Make sure your objective is specific and relates to the position for which you are applying.
- Make sure everything on your résumé relates back to the objective.
- Whenever possible, showcase transferable skills.
- Include achievements as well as duties and responsibilities when delineating work experience.
- Demonstrate that you have the necessary skills to perform the job.
- Categorize your experience and skills so it can be easily understood by the reader.
- Keep the résumé to one page in length, if possible.
- Use adequate "white space." A sheet of paper with text covering every printable space is difficult to read and looks cluttered, unfriendly, and uninviting.
- Bold and underline sparingly and consistently.
- Make sure vertical and horizontal spacing is consistent with 1" margins on all sides.
- Have someone proofread your resume before sending it out.
- Bullet items rather than numbering or lettering them.
- Use action verbs when identifying duties and responsibilities.

SHORT LIST OF ACTION VERBS

Accelerated	Directed	Increased
Accomplished	Established	Initiated
Administered	Executed	Introduced
Analyzed	Expanded	Launched
Compiled	Founded	Managed
Converted	Generated	Organized
Created	Improved	Planned
Designed	Reduced	Trained
Developed	Researched	Transformed

** Note: *Look for "keywords" in the Job Description, or the Want Ad, and use these words (only if applicable to you) in your résumé.*

DON'TS

- Title your résumé: "Résumé" or "Curriculum Vitae."
- List references on your résumé or include the statement "References Upon Request."
- Indicate a salary requirement on your résumé.
- Use abbreviations—state abbreviations and academic titles are acceptable.
- Provide personal information about marital status, religious affiliation, health, etc.
- Use the word "I" in the résumé. (May be used in your cover letter.)
- Lie or exaggerate on a résumé. Everything you write down can be checked and verified.

The following pages include a layout for a combination résumé, and examples of functional, chronological, and combination résumés.

Layout for a Combination Résumé

HEADING

Your name
Address
Telephone
Email

OBJECTIVE: Position you are looking for within the company, type of job; industry; location

EDUCATION: Last school attended listed first.
Name of school, city, state, degree awarded, honors, GPA (if 3.0 or higher)

PROFESSIONAL QUALIFICATIONS: Skills that will make you stand out from other candidates. Ex. Fluent in Foreign language or Sign Language, Adobe Photoshop, Excel, Access, Publisher.
- Fluent in Spanish, French
- Skilled in Adobe Photoshop

WORK EXPERIENCE: Most current position listed first.

Job title, name of company, city, state, dates of employment
- Duties/responsibilities- Use action verbs ...Coordinated... Developed.. Managed..
- Duties/responsibilities -Use action verbs ...Coordinated... Developed.. Managed..
- Duties/responsibilities -Use action verbs ...Coordinated... Developed.. Managed..
- Duties/responsibilities -Use action verbs ...Coordinated... Developed.. Managed..
- Duties/responsibilities -Use action verbs ...Coordinated... Developed.. Managed..

COMMUNITY SERVICE/
PROFESSIONAL AFFILIATIONS/
ACCOMPLISHMENTS:

Sample Functional Résumé

JAMES JONES
1423 Mercy Drive
Detroit, MI 56972
981-456-1235
JJ445@earthlink.net

OBJECTIVE:

Sales management position in a large car dealership in the metro Chicago area, that utilizes my experience to increase sales and profits for the company.

EXPERIENCE:

Management	Directed and trained 40 representatives in sales and customer service skills, created quality control programs, and reduced employee turnover rates.
Sales Representative	Increased sales of luxury cars at dealerships throughout west Michigan; successfully introduced two car lines; trained and motivated sales team of twelve, to increase productivity.
Public Relations	Designed artistic advertising for major retail company; developed marketing materials; wrote press releases.
Training	Supervised training procedures for office personnel; created training manual for all new sales employees; taught sales and retailing at a local community college.

EMPLOYMENT HISTORY:

1997 to present	**Sales manager.** Mitchell's Advertising Aeencv, Detroit, MI
1992- 1997	**Personnel and Public Relations Director.** Donnie Deutsch Designs, Duluth, MN
1985-1992	**Sales clerk.** Bloominadale's, New York, NY.

EDUCATION:

1981-1992	New York University, New York, NY. Bachelors of Arts in Advertising & Public Relations.
1977-1981	Art & Design High School, New York, NY. Major: Advertising/ Illustration

Sample Chronological Résumé

MELINDA GREGORAVICH
22-51 90th Street
East Elmhurst, NY 11370
212-445-0000
melgreg@aol.com

OBJECTIVE:

To teach political science and history at a post-secondary level college in the New York area.

WORK HISTORY:

May 2005-present **Faculty/Advisor**, New York School of Technology, New York, NY

- Taught United States Federal Government, American history courses.
- Advised freshmen students on course enrollment.
- Served on faculty senate.

January 2004-January 2005 **Instructor**, La Costa Junior College, La Costa, CA

- Taught political science, world history, and psychology courses.
- Served as faculty advisor to students in Phi Beta Kappa society.

September 2001-December 2003 **Graduate Assistant**, California State University, Fullerton, CA

- Taught Psychology 101 course.
- Assisted in grading papers, developing course curriculum.

EDUCATION:

December 2003   California State University, Fullerton, CA., MA - Political Science
May 2000   University of Miami, Miami, FL, BS – History

SKILLS:

- Proficient in MS Word, Excel, PowerPoint
- Fluent in Spanish, Italian

APPENDIX: Résumé/Cover Letters/Interviewing Process

Sample Combination Résumé

SARAH SMILE
555 Main Street
City, State Zip
(xxx) xxx-xxxx
Sarahsmile@,anywhere.com

OBJECTIVE

Seeking a full-time *customer service* position with a small marketing corporation located in the Metro Orlando area, that will utilize my extensive office management and computer related skills.

PROFESSIONAL QUALIFICATIONS

- Experience with using the entire MS Office Suite including Word, Excel, Access, and PowerPoint.
- Performed mass e-mailing using the combined functions of MS Word and Outlook.
- Developed and used complex multi-page Excel spreadsheets to perform calculations, maintain records, monitor costs, and track performance of individuals.
- Used the Internet to perform work related research.
- Developed and implemented a new filing system which reduced lost files by 98%.

WORK EXPERIENCE

Technical Support Representative, Team Leader, NPI Training
Convergvs, Heathrow, FL - October 2005--Present
- Provide technical support to customers.
- Troubleshoot computer networking problems.
- Train customer service representatives.
- Defuse complex customer service issues.
- Inform team members of new products lines and related support issues.

Office Manager, Admissions Department
Rollins College, Sanford, FL - August 2003-October 2005
- Tracked four budgets for director in excess of $3,000,000.
- Maximized office productivity through proficient use of appropriate software applications.
- Trained new staff members.
- Formulated procedures for systematic retention, protection, retrieval, transfer, and disposal of records.

EDUCATION

General Education (AA)

Seminole Community College, *Sanford, FL - 2003-2005*
- 3.83 GPA on 4.0 Scale

Graduated with honors and distinction December 2005

COMMUNITY SERVICE

Volunteered with Habitat for Humanity to build homes for local disadvantaged.

Writing a Cover Letter

There are three parts to the content portion of a cover letter.

1. Introductory Paragraph

The first paragraph in a cover letter should state your interest in applying for the position, explain how you learned about the opportunity, and express your desire about the prospect of working for the organization.

2. Middle Paragraph(s)

The middle paragraph(s) should highlight the knowledge, skills, and abilities that you would bring to the position. The information you present should also demonstrate how you would meet the company's needs. Although you may have included some of the same skills on your résumé, they should be reiterated in your cover letter with slightly different wording. This is an opportunity to show off your writing skills—a skill that all employers are looking for in their employees.

In this section, you can also address any "negative flags," which you were not able to conceal in the résumé (i.e., a long absence from the workplace and school). You want to show the employer how your previous experiences can be tied in with the skills needed for the position. Be certain that your résumé and cover letter are congruent. For example, any dates of employment, specific employers, or work experiences that are cited in the cover letter should also appear in your résumé.

3. Closing Paragraph

The closing paragraph should indicate your desire and availability for an interview. Be sure to provide your current contact information. Thank the reader for his or her time and consideration, and indicate that you are looking forward to a reply.

Helpful hints: Although the word "I" can be used in your cover letter, avoid using it excessively at the beginning of a sentence or paragraph. Visit your local career center, or various career websites for sample cover letters. There are also several software programs that contain cover letter templates and samples. The following page illustrates a template for writing a cover letter.

Cover Letter Template

Your name
Your address

Date
Name of Company/Organization
Name of Division or Search Committee
Address
City, State, Zip

Salutation (e.g. Dear Mr. Doe or Dear Search Committee Chairperson:)

First paragraph:
State your interest, and describe the position you are seeking with the organization. Cite how you learned about the opportunity (online, newspaper, word of mouth).

Second Paragraph:
State your qualifications for the position. Mention one or two achievements (if they are relevant) to the job you are seeking. Do not reiterate <u>everything</u> that is on the resume.

Closing Paragraph:
Bring attention to the enclosed résumé; request an interview; state how you can be contacted.

Complimentary close and signature:
(e.g. Sincerely, Cordially)

Nancy Drew

Enclosure

The Interviewing Process

PREPARING FOR THE INTERVIEW

Congratulations! You have sent off your wonderfully prepared résumé and it has landed you an interview with an employer. Now what do you do? How do you make the most of this opportunity to sell yourself to the employer?

It is important for you to keep a log of the companies that have scheduled you for interview appointments. This is particularly wise to do if you have sent out a large number of résumés. Find a method (paper or electronic) to write down the name of the company, the position you are seeking, phone number of the company, contact person, and the date of the interview.

The interview session is the final component in landing you a job. Remember to arrive on time for the interview session and conduct yourself in a professional manner.

DO YOUR RESEARCH

Before you go on an interview, do some research on the company and the position for which you are applying. There are many resources available to obtain information about the field of work, the specific company, and the position. Here are some suggestions:

- **Company's Website**
- **Annual Report.** The annual report of a company tells you how they are doing financially, and the diversity of the company's assets.
- **Occupational Outlook Handbook.** Published by the United States Department of Labor, the handbook gives descriptive information about careers, as well as a ten-year projection on job availability. The Handbook is revised every two years.
- **Dictionary of Occupational Titles.** The dictionary describes the duties and physical demands of a variety of careers.
- www.salary.com. This website can give you the salary range on a variety of careers.

DRESS FOR SUCCESS

In the social intelligence section, we spoke about nonverbal communication. The way you present yourself in an interview, from your choice of clothing to your expressions, speaks volumes about your confidence and your understanding of the culture of the workplace.

Suggestions for Female Applicants
- **Hairstyle should be attractive and under control.**
  Big, bushy hair or fly-away hair does not convey professionalism.
- **Wear minimal makeup.**
  Make sure your makeup is understated. Use just enough makeup to enhance your features.
- **Wear moderate jewelry.**
  Keep your jewelry simple. Too much jewelry can be distracting to an interviewer.
- **Clean your fingernails; avoid chipped polish.**
  If you wear polish, make sure it is a traditional color. The safest polish is clear or a French manicure.
- **Wear conservative hosiery.**
  Hosiery should be a neutral color. Avoid wearing fashionable hosiery (fishnets).
- **Wear a conservative, but stylish suit.**
  Female candidates should wear a conservative, but stylish suit. Avoid wearing miniskirts or low-cut blouses. **Note:** Wearing a very conservative suit may not be appropriate if you are applying for a position in a creative industry (i.e., art director, interior designer).
- **Wear conservative shoes.**
  Wear a conservative closed toe and closed heel dress shoe. Make sure your shoes are in good condition and polished. Avoid stilettos or casual footwear.
- **Carry either a portfolio or attaché case.**
  Make sure your pen and paper are easily accessible.
- **If possible, conceal any tattoos.**

Suggestions for Male Applicants
- **Make sure hair is clean and recently trimmed.**
  Facial hair should be at a minimum. However, if you have facial hair, be sure it is freshly trimmed.
- **Wear a conservative, but stylish suit.**
  The color should be a traditional black, navy, or dark tweed. The shirt and tie should be a complement to the conservative suit. **NOTE:** Interviewing for a position in a creative industry allows for less conservative attire.

- **Clean and trim your nails.**
  Ensure that your nails are clean and trimmed. Visible dirt under fingernails, or nails that are uneven and ragged, could hinder your chances of being employed.
- **Wear appropriate, clean shoes**.
  A traditional business style shoe would be the best choice to wear. Make sure that they are shined and in good repair.
- **Store a minimum amount of things in pockets.**
  Do not fill your pocket with large sets of keys, coins, or an overly packed wallet. Bulging pockets will give you an unprofessional appearance.
- **Wear matching socks.**
  Be sure to check (using adequate lighting) that you have selected a matching pair of socks. Socks should match the traditional suit color – black, navy, or dark tweed.
- **Wear minimal jewelry**.
  Keep jewelry to a minimum. Avoid wearing gold chains or garish diamond jewelry. Remove all jewelry from body piercings.
- **If possible, conceal any tattoos**.

CONTACTING YOUR REFERENCES

It is important that you contact your references in advance, to inform them that they may be contacted by the prospective employer. Give your references information about the company and the position you are seeking. If possible, send each of your references a copy of your most recent résumé.

CATEGORIES OF INTERVIEW QUESTIONS

During the interview, you will be asked a number of questions. The questions are designed to draw out information about your performance in the workplace, and may include some of the following areas:

- **Oral Communication**
  The success of the entire interview could rest on your ability to communicate your ideas effectively.
- **Written Communication**
  To assess writing skills, many employers ask applicants to do a writing sample as part of the interview process.

- **Decision Making**
  Interviewers will often ask you to describe an instance when you had to make a business decision and the impact of that decision. Be prepared to recite an example of your decision-making skills.
- **Motivation**
  Prospective employers want to know how you motivate others and how you motivate yourself. Once again, be ready to give a specific example related to motivation.
- **Leadership**
  Interviewers often ask the applicant to describe a situation where they took the lead on a project.
- **Interpersonal Skills**
  A question that is often asked in interviews is: How would you handle an angry customer? The interviewer is trying to gain insight into your interpersonal skills, so be prepared to field the "angry customer" question.
- **Planning and Organization**
  Be prepared to describe a situation that reflects your planning and organizational skills.
- **Teamwork**
  Give examples from your past work experiences that show you are a team player. Try to be specific. Vague answers can create questions in the interviewer's mind as to whether you really are a team player.
- **Diversity**
  In the twenty-first century, diversity has become a vital issue. We live in a global society. You will often be asked to share your view of diversity. Diversity is about race, gender, sexual preference, disabilities, and religious preference.
- **Problem Solving**
  Problem solving is a very important employability skill. You may be asked to describe a time or situation when you had to solve a complex problem. Be prepared to explain the steps you took to solve the problem.

MOCK INTERVIEW OPPORTUNITY

It is a good idea to practice your interviewing skills. Your local college career center, or your local library, may have software programs on interviewing skills, which you can utilize to practice your skills.

An example of one of these software programs is **The Perfect Interview**. The Perfect Interview is an innovative software program that uses webcam technology to assist users in developing their interviewing skills. The program asks a variety of interview questions at varying levels of difficulty and then records the user's response using a webcam. In addition, the program provides coaching for each question by a seasoned professional, and provides an example of an appropriate response.

QUESTIONS YOU SHOULD BE PREPARED TO ASK THE INTERVIEWER

Once you have answered all of the interviewer's questions, there is generally some time left for you to ask questions of the interviewer. So make sure you have a few good questions to ask. These questions should not be frivolous. You need to give thought to your choice of questions, and show that you are a serious candidate who has given serious consideration to the position and organization. For example, you can ask for clarification about some of the details of the job. Limit your questions to no more than six. Here are some sample questions:

1. What are some of the goals projected for this department in the coming year?
2. How are employees evaluated?
3. What major contributions do you expect from this position?
4. What qualifications would the ideal candidate have for this job?
5. What have been the greatest organizational challenges in the past year?
6. Is there a staff development program?
7. What do you see as the company's greatest assets/weaknesses?
8. How would you describe the organizational culture?
9. What makes this organization different from its competitors?
10. What is the typical career path of someone who starts in this position?

AFTER THE INTERVIEW

Thank-You Letter

It is considered good business etiquette to send a thank-you letter to the employer after you have completed your interview. It provides you with another opportunity to sell yourself, correct any mistakes you think you made in the formal interview, and show your written communication skills. The thank-you letter should be sent within 24 hours of the interview, and can be sent via mail, fax, or e-mail.

authors' biographies

Patricia Ferguson has a doctorate degree in Curriculum and Instruction and a master's degree in Counselor Education. She has over two decades of professional experience at the community college and university levels assisting students with "finding their bliss." She is a founding member of Counseling, Courage and Careers, an organization dedicated to bringing life and career skills to the community. She was born and raised in Akron, Ohio, and currently resides with her family in Florida.

Victoria Nanos has a master's degree in College Counseling and Student Development. She has over twenty years' experience as a counselor at both the community college and university levels. Ms. Nanos has taught Theories of Personality, Child Psychology, and Life Career Planning courses at the college level. She was born in Brockton, Massachusetts, and raised in New York City. She currently resides in Florida and is living her "bliss" as a sculptor.